"'一带一路'与粤港澳大湾区特色教材"研究成果

实用交际汉语 1

Practical Communicative Chinese

王功平　李贤卓　编著

北京语言大学出版社
BEIJING LANGUAGE AND CULTURE
UNIVERSITY PRESS

图书在版编目（CIP）数据

实用交际汉语. 1 / 王功平，李贤卓编著. —北京：北京语言大学出版社，2023.7

ISBN 978-7-5619-6245-9

I. ①实… II. ①王… ②李… III. ①汉语－口语－对外汉语教学－教材 IV. ①H195.4

中国国家版本馆 CIP 数据核字 (2023) 第 110481 号

实用交际汉语 1

SHIYONG JIAOJI HANYU 1

版式设计：邱　彬　黄　莉
排版制作：北京青侣文化创意设计有限公司
图片提供：王功平　壹图网
责任印制：周　燚

出版发行：北京语言大学出版社
社　　址：北京市海淀区学院路 15 号，100083
网　　址：www.blcup.com
电子信箱：service@blcup.com
电　　话：编辑部　8610-82303647/3592/3395
国内发行　8610-82303650/3591/3648
海外发行　8610-82303365/3080/3668
北语书店　8610-82303653
网购咨询　8610-82303908
印　　刷：北京鑫丰华彩印有限公司

版　　次：2023 年 7 月第 1 版　　印　　次：2023 年 7 月第 1 次印刷
开　　本：787 毫米 × 1092 毫米　1/16　　印　　张：16.75
字　　数：198 千字
定　　价：68.00 元

PRINTED IN CHINA
凡有印装质量问题，本社负责调换。售后QQ号1367565611，电话010-82303590

前言

《实用交际汉语》是“‘一带一路’与粤港澳大湾区特色教材”的研究成果。本套教材以培养汉语学习者的汉语交际能力为核心，侧重面向“一带一路”国家的初级汉语学习者。教材既适用于正式在校的学习者，也适用于补习班或者个人辅导班的学习者；既适用于初学汉语的中小学生，也适用于广大成人初级汉语学习者。

全套教材共 4 册。考虑到有的海外国家采用一年三学期制，每学期除了节日和复习考试外，实际上课 12 周，同时考虑到不同学校开设汉语课的周学时有差异，我们按照平均每周 2 次课、每次 2 个课时的教学时间安排内容。每册共计 24 课，包括 6 大项 24 小项的交际功能和两个综合实践训练。这些交际功能包括“见面问候”“请求帮助”“购物讲价”“体育健身”“看病就医”“旅游观光”等，可以满足学习者日常生活、学习和出行的常用交际需求。

本套教材在编写过程中主要遵循如下思路：

采用意验大纲

教材的编写既突破早期以字词为纲的理念，也突破后来以结构（语法）为纲的理念，同时还突破以功能（交际功能）为纲的理念，主要采用意验大纲，同时兼顾字词和语法的难度等级。这里的“意验”主要指学习者跟随本教材学习汉语的过程，也是运用汉语发展交际意识、体验交际功能和文化的过程。比如，学习者通过学习第一册的第一至三课及第十课，就可以掌握在不同场合中与不同年龄、身份的人见面时打招呼的方式；同时，在学习过程中体验打招呼的不同方式之间的汉语用语差异。其中，第一课安排的交际功能为生人之间的见面及问候，第二、三课安排的交际功能为熟人之间的见面及问候，而第十课安排的交际功能则为在正式场合下礼貌地询问他人姓名的方式。这样的次序又兼顾了字词、语法、功能和文化的难易程度。

紧紧围绕一个目标

教材坚持以培养学习者的汉语交际能力为核心，让学习者多层次、全方位地了解中国，包括中国的历史和现状，中国的社会、经济、科技、文化等各个领域的发展情况。

坚持两翼并举

教材坚持听力和口语两大技能齐头并进，以听带说，以说促听。

努力做到三驾齐驱

教材努力做到语言、文化和科技三驾齐驱，以掌握语言（汉语）为基础，以了解文化为目标，以科学的载体为推进器，适应移动学习（M-Learning）、即时学习（Just-in-Time Learning）、掌上学习（P-Learning）的需求。

切实实现五管齐下

（1）交际性。每课话题的选取、语法点的讲解、文化点的介绍、课后练习的设计都紧紧围绕“提高学习者的汉语交际能力”这一核心目标。（2）真实性。教材中课文的语料均来源于真实的生活，服务于真实的交际场景。（3）适用性。教材适用于不同母语或第一语言背景及不同汉语水平的学习者。（4）科学性。教材的所有生词、语法点和交际话题的选取、排序，均参考了学界的权威大纲，比如《汉语水平等级标准与语法等级大纲》、《高等学校外国留学生汉语言专业教学大纲》（附件二）、《国际汉语教学通用课程大纲》及《国际中文教育中文水平等级标准》等。(5)趣味性。主要包括内容的趣味性和形式的趣味性，不同的课文相互衔接成完整的故事，学习者可以在“交”(交际)中学，也可以在学中“交”(交际)。

协调好五大关系

(1)中与外的关系。教材内容不全是关于中国的，也有关于世界其他国家的，比如世界杯、母亲节等，以增强对学习者的亲和力。(2)古与今的关系。教材内容既介绍了中国古代的成就，也讲述了中国当今社会的方方面面。(3)语与文的关系。语言和文化紧密相连，水乳交融，相互促进。教材每课都配备一个与本课内容相关的“文化小常识”，方便学习者在学习汉语的同时，更深入地了解中国文化。(4)学与用的关系。教材注重使学习者在学中用，以用促学；让学习者感到学有所用，用有所得，学起来轻松，用起来顺手。(5)俗与雅的关系。教材的内容既包括通俗的日常交际话题和用语，也包括文雅的正式交际话题和用语。

教材的体例安排如下：每课均在标题下给出该课的学习重点提示，主要内容则包括看图讨论、课文对话、生词注释、主要语言点讲解、文化小常识介绍、练习与实践六大部分。其中，看图讨论部分图文并茂，紧扣主题，抛砖引玉。课文内容真实、生动，人物对话既独立成篇，又注意有机统一、前后连贯。各课之间相互联系，环环相扣，引人入胜。对话交际项目的选取，既遵循学习者由易到难的学习规律，又符合社会发展趋势，紧扣时代脉搏。主要语言点讲解部分重点突出，句法、语义、语用结合，尤其突出交际功能的讲解。例句简单、实用，并附动画视频，可使学生身临其境地体验交际场景。文化小常识介绍以点带面，重点突出，系统全面。练习与实践部分题型灵活，形式多样，内容丰富，既紧扣课文，又有拓展及延伸，与课文形成阶梯式爬坡，以满足不同水平学习者的需要。

本套教材的特色在于：(1)以先进的语言教学理论为指导，尤其注重吸收国际上先进的二语教学理念和教材编写理论。(2)有丰富的习得研究成果和教学经验的支撑，切实做到融汉语知识体系、二语习得规律和汉语教学经验于一炉。（3）交际话题具有真实性、实用性，教材所有话题均源于实践，并且加以条理化、系统化。（4）灵活运用新技术，打造多媒体资源支持的立体化教材。教材配以丰富的图片、录音、动画视频及汉字动态书写演示图等丰富的学习资源，以保证课堂教学真实化、生活化，学生课后复习自主化、随时化。

我们还将为教材的使用者（包括汉语学习者和国际汉语教师）提供灵活多样的教材使用服务，包括提供配套的汉字、语法学习资源，为汉语教师提供适用的教学课件，并适时组织相关教师进行教材使用培训和教学指导等。

为使本套教材能更好地服务广大汉语学习者和国际汉语教师，恳请大家在使用过程中提出宝贵的意见和建议。各位朋友递送意见或建议的联系方式为：1922418845@qq.com（电子邮箱）、pingw0159（微信号）。

编者

2023 年 3 月

目 录

交际项目六 换钱购物

综合实践二

预备课

Preparatory Lesson

汉语语音简介

Introduction to Chinese Phonetics

汉语大多数音节都由声母、韵母和声调三个部分组成。音节开头的辅音是声母，其后的部分是韵母，韵母上面的标号是声调（轻声不标声调）。例如：bà（爸）这个音节中，b 是声母，a 是韵母，a 上面的标号“ˋ”是声调。

Most Chinese syllables are formed of three parts: the initial, the final and the tone. The consonant at the beginning of a syllable is the initial, the rest of the syllable is the final, and the label on the final is the tone (except for the neutral tone, which is not marked). For example, in bà, b is the initial, a is the final, and the label at the top of a is the tone.

汉语声母多数是清辅音，浊辅音做声母的只有 m、n、l、r 四个。汉语没有复辅音（即两个辅音相连）。

Most Chinese initials are voiceless consonants. Only four voiced consonants are used as initials, i.e., m, n, l, and r, and there are no compound consonants (that is, two consonants combined into one) in Chinese.

汉语每一个音节必须有韵母，任何一个韵母必须有一个或一个以上的元音。

Every Chinese syllable must have a final, and any final must have one or more vowels.

汉语有四个声调：一声 ˉ 、二声 ˊ 、三声ˇ、四声 ˋ 。

Chinese has four tones: the first tone, the second tone, the third tone, and the fourth tone.

一、声母 Chinese initials

汉语普通话共有21个声母（不包括零声母）。这些不同声母的主要区别在于发音部位和发音方法不同。

There are 21 initials in Mandarin Chinese (not including zero initials). The main difference among these initials lies in the place of articulation and the pronunciation methods.

按发音部位（即发音时，阻碍气流的器官位置）的不同，声母可以分为双唇音、唇齿音、舌尖前音、舌尖中音、舌尖后音、舌面音和舌根音七大类。

According to the place of articulation (that is, the position of the organ that obstructs the air stream during pronunciation), initials can be classified into seven categories: bilabials, labiodentals, frontal-alveolars, alveolars, post-alveolars, palatals and velars.

声母的发音方法又可从三个方面来区分：阻碍气流的方式、声带是否振动、气流的强弱。

The pronunciation methods of initials can be distinguished from three aspects: the way of obstructing the air stream, the vocal cords vibrating or not, and the strength of the air stream.

根据发音时阻碍气流的方式，声母可以分为塞音、塞擦音、擦音、鼻音和边音五大类。

According to the way in which the air stream is obstructed during pronunciation, initials can be classified into five categories: plosives, affricates, fricatives, nasals and laterals.

根据发音时声带是否振动，声母可以分为浊音（振动）和清音（不振动）两大类。

According to whether the vocal cords vibrate during pronunciation, initials can be classified into two categories: voiced initials (vibrating) and voiceless initials (not vibrating).

根据发音时气流的强弱，声母可以分为送气音（气流强）和不送气音（气流弱）两大类。

According to the strength of the air stream during pronunciation, initials can be classified into two categories: aspirated initials (strong air stream) and unaspirated initials (weak air stream).

汉语普通话 21 个声母的发音部位和发音方法可以归纳为表 1。

The articulation places and pronunciation methods of the 21 Mandarin Chinese initials can be summarized in Table 1 below.

表 1　汉语普通话声母总表

发音方法		双唇音		唇齿音	舌尖前音	舌尖中音		舌尖后音		舌面音	舌根音
		清音	浊音	清音	清音	清音	浊音	清音	浊音	清音	清音
塞音	不送气	b [p]				d [t]					g [k]
	送气	p [p^h]				t [t^h]					k [k^h]
塞擦音	不送气				z [ts]			zh [tʂ]		j [tɕ]	
	送气				c [ts^h]			ch [tʂ^h]		q [tɕ^h]	
擦 音				f [f]	s [s]			sh [ʂ]	r [ʐ]	x [ɕ]	h [x]
鼻 音			m[m]				n [n]				
边 音							l [l]				

汉语普通话各个声母的发音要点如下：

The keywords for the articulation of each initial in Mandarin Chinese are as follows:

b [p]: 双唇、不送气、清、塞音。

b [p]: bilabial; unaspirated; voiceless; plosive.

p [p^h]: 双唇、送气、清、塞音。

p [p^h]: bilabial; aspirated; voiceless; plosive.

m [m]: 双唇、浊、鼻音。

m [m]: bilabial; voiced; nasal.

f [f]：唇齿、清、擦音。

f [f]: labiodental; voiceless; fricative.

d [t]：舌尖中、不送气、清、塞音。

d [t]: alveolar; unaspirated; voiceless; plosive.

t [tʰ]：舌尖中、送气、清、塞音。

t [tʰ]: alveolar; aspirated; voiceless; plosive.

n [n]：舌尖中、浊、鼻音。

n [n]: alveolar; voiced; nasal.

l [l]：舌尖中、浊、边音。

l [l]: alveolar; voiced; lateral.

j [tɕ]：舌面、不送气、清、塞擦音。

j [tɕ]: palatal; unaspirated; voiceless; affricate.

q [tɕʰ]：舌面、送气、清、塞擦音。

q [tɕʰ]: palatal; aspirated; voiceless; affricate.

x [ɕ]：舌面、清、擦音。

x [ɕ]: palatal; voiceless; fricative.

g [k]：舌根、不送气、清、塞音。

g [k]: velar; unaspirated; voiceless; plosive.

k [kʰ]：舌根、送气、清、塞音。

k [kʰ]: velar; aspirated; voiceless; plosive.

h [x]：舌根、清、擦音。

h [x]: velar; voiceless; fricative.

z [ts]：舌尖前、不送气、清、塞擦音

z [ts]: frontal-alveolar; unaspirated; voiceless; affricate.

c [tsʰ]：舌尖前、送气、清、塞擦音。

c [tsʰ]: frontal-alveolar; aspirated; voiceless; affricate.

s [s]：舌尖前、清、擦音。

s [s]: frontal-alveolar; voiceless; fricative.

zh [tʂ]：舌尖后、不送气、清、塞擦音。

zh [tʂ]: post-alveolar; unaspirated; voiceless; affricate.

ch [tʂʰ]：舌尖后、送气、清、塞擦音。

ch [tʂʰ]: post-alveolar; aspirated; voiceless; affricate.

sh [ʂ]：舌尖后、清、擦音。

sh [ʂ]: post-alveolar; voiceless; fricative.

r [ʐ]：舌尖后、浊、擦音。

r [ʐ]: post-alveolar; voiced; fricative.

二、汉语韵母 Chinese finals

汉语普通话有 39 个韵母，有的韵母由元音构成，如 ɑ、iɑ、iɑo；有的韵母由元音加辅音构成，如 ɑn、iɑn、iɑng。元音必不可少。

There are 39 finals in Mandarin Chinese. Some finals are formed by one or several vowels, for example, ɑ, iɑ, iɑo; some finals are combinations of vowels and consonants, for example, ɑn, iɑn, iɑng. Vowels are essential.

普通话的韵母按照结构可以分成三大类：单元音韵母、复元音韵母和带鼻音韵母。

The finals of Mandarin Chinese can be classified into three categories according to their structures: single finals, compound finals, and nasal finals.

1. 单元音韵母 Single finals

单元音韵母就是由一个元音构成的韵母。不同单元音韵母的发音特点主要表现在参与发音的器官（主要是舌头）在口腔中的高低和前后位置，以及口型（主要是嘴唇）的圆展三个方面。我们可以从上述三个方面将这些不同的单元音韵母分类，如表 2 所示。学习这些单元音韵母时，主要应注意这三个方面。

Single finals are those formed by one vowel. The pronunciation characteristics of different single finals are mainly manifested in three aspects: the high-low and front-back positions of the organs involved in the articulation (mainly the tongue), as well as the roundness/flatness of the mouth shape (mainly the lips). Chinese single finals can be classified according to the above three aspects as shown in Table 2. When learning these single finals, we should also focus our attention on these three aspects.

表 2　汉语普通话单元音韵母总表

舌位高低	舌面元音					舌尖元音		卷舌元音
	前元音		央元音	后元音		前元音	后元音	央元音
	唇形不圆	唇形圆	唇形自然	唇形不圆	唇形圆	唇形不圆	唇形不圆	唇形自然
最高元音	i [i]	ü [y]			u [u]	-i [ɿ]	-i [ʅ]	
半高元音				e [ɤ]	o [o]			
正中								er [ər]
半低元音	ê [ɛ]							
最低元音			ɑ [A]					

2. 复元音韵母　Compound finals

由两个或两个以上的元音构成的韵母叫复元音韵母。复元音韵母可以分为韵头、韵腹和韵尾三个部分，其中韵头和韵尾可以没有，但韵腹不可少。

Compound finals are combinations of two or more vowels. A compound final can be divided into three parts: the head, the abdomen and the tail. The head and the tail can be missing, but the abdomen is indispensable.

3. 带鼻音韵母　Nasal finals

韵母带鼻辅音 n 或 ng 的韵母叫作带鼻音韵母。

A nasal final is the one that ends with the nasal consonant n or ng.

表 3 为汉语普通话的韵母总表。

See Table 3 for the comprehensive classification of all Chinese finals.

表 3 汉语普通话韵母总表

类型	开头（第一个）元音的特点				韵尾情况
	开口呼	齐齿呼	合口呼	撮口呼	
单元音韵母（10）	-i [ɿ] -i [ʅ]	i [i]	u [u]	ü [y]	无韵尾韵母（15）
	ɑ [A]				
	o [o]				
	e [ɤ]				
	ê [ɛ]				
	er [ər]				
复元音韵母（13）		iɑ [iA]	uɑ [uA]		
			uo [uo]		
		ie [iɛ]		üe [yɛ]	
	ɑi [ai]		uɑi [uai]		元音韵尾韵母（8）
	ei [ei]		uei [uei]		
	ɑo [ɑu]	iɑo [iɑu]			
	ou [ou]	iou [iou]			
带鼻音韵母（16）	ɑn [an]	iɑn [iɛn]	uɑn [uan]	üɑn [yan]	鼻音韵尾韵母（16）
	en [ən]	in [in]	uen [uən]	ün [yn]	
	ɑng [ɑŋ]	iɑng [iɑŋ]	uɑng [uɑŋ]		
	eng [əŋ]	ing [iŋ]	ueng [uəŋ]		
			ong [uŋ]	iong [yŋ]	

普通话各个韵母的发音要点如下：

The keywords for the articulation of each final in Mandarin are as follows:

ɑ [A]：舌面、央、低、不圆唇元音。

ɑ [A]: palatal; central; low; unrounded.

o [o]：舌面、后、半高、圆唇元音。

o [o]: palatal; back; half-high; rounded.

e [ɤ]：舌面、后、半高、不圆唇元音。

e [ɤ]: palatal; back; half-high; unrounded.

ê [ɛ]：舌面、前、半低、不圆唇元音。

ê [ɛ]: palatal; front; half-low; unrounded.

u [u]：舌面、后、高、圆唇元音。

u [u]: palatal; back; high; rounded.

ü [y]：舌面、前、高、圆唇元音。

ü [y]: palatal; front; high; rounded.

i [i]：舌面、前、高、不圆唇元音。

i [i]: palatal; front; high; unrounded.

-i [ɿ]：舌尖、前、高、不圆唇元音。

-i [ɿ]: alveolar; front; high; unrounded.

-i [ʅ]：舌尖、后、高、不圆唇元音。

-i [ʅ]: alveolar; back; high; unrounded.

er [ər]：卷舌、央、中、不圆唇元音。

er [ər]: retroflex; central; middle; unrounded.

ɑi [ai]：先发 ɑ [a] 音，然后滑向发 i [i] 音。注意这里 ɑ [a] 的舌位比单元音 ɑ [A] 的偏前一点儿，并且 ɑ [a] 比 i [i] 要发得重些、长些。

When pronouncing ɑi [ai], the tongue position and mouth shape naturally slide from those of a [a] to those of i [i]. Note that the tongue position of a [a] here is a little more to the forward than the single vowel a [A], and a [a] is pronounced heavier and longer than i [i].

ei [ei]：先发 e [e] 音，然后滑向发 i [i] 音。注意 e [e] 比 i [i] 要发得重些、长些。

When pronouncing ei [ei] , the tongue position and mouth shape naturally slide from those of e [e] to those of i [i]. Note that e [e] is pronounced heavier and longer than i [i].

ao [ɑu]：先发 a [ɑ] 音，然后滑向发 o [u] 音。注意这里 a [ɑ] 的舌位比单元音的 a [A] 的偏后一点儿，并且 a [ɑ] 比 o [u] 要发得重些、长些。

When pronouncing ao [ɑu], the tongue position and mouth shape naturally slide from those of a [ɑ] to those of o [u]. Note that the tongue position of a [ɑ] here is a little more to the back than the single vowel a [A], and a [ɑ] is pronounced heavier and longer than o [u].

ou [ou]：先发 o [o] 音，然后滑向发 u [u] 音。注意 o [o] 比 u [u] 要发得重些、长些。

When pronouncing ou [ou], the tongue position and mouth shape naturally slide from those of o [o] to those of u [u]. Note that o [o] is pronounced heavier and longer than u [u].

ie [iɛ]：先发 i [i]，然后转向发 e [ɛ]。注意这里的 e 发 [ɛ]，并且 e [ɛ] 比 i [i] 要发得重些、长些。

When pronouncing ie [iɛ] , the tongue position and mouth shape naturally slide from those of i [i] to those of e [ɛ]. Note that e is pronounced [ɛ] here, and it is pronounced heavier and longer than i [i].

üe [yɛ]：先发 ü [y] 音，然后转向发 e [ɛ] 音。注意这里的 e 发 [ɛ]，并且 e [ɛ] 比 ü [y] 要发得重些、长些。

When pronouncing üe [yɛ], the tongue position and mouth shape naturally slide from those of ü [y] to those of e [ɛ]. Note that e is pronounced [ɛ] here, and it is pronounced heavier and longer than ü [y].

ia [iA]：先发 i [i] 音，然后转向发 a [A] 音。注意这里的 a 发 [A]，并且 a [A] 比 i [i] 要发得重些、长些。

When pronouncing ia [iA], the tongue position and mouth shape naturally slide from those of i [i] to those of a [A]. Note that a is pronounced [A] here, and it is pronounced heavier and longer than i [i].

ua [uA]：先发 u [u] 的音，然后转向发 a [A] 音。注意这里的 a 发 [A]，并且 a [A] 比 u [u] 要发得重些、长些。

When pronouncing ua [uA], the tongue position and mouth shape naturally slide from those of u [u] to those of a [A]. Note that a is pronounced [A] here, and it is pronounced heavier and longer than u [u].

uo [uo]：先发 u [u] 的音，然后转向发 o [o] 音。注意 o [o] 比 u [u] 要发得重些、长些。

When pronouncing uo [uo], the tongue position and mouth shape naturally slide from those of u [u] to those of o [o]. Note that o [o] is pronounced heavier and longer than u [u].

iou [iou]：先发 i [i] 音，然后滑向发 o [o] 音，最后转到发 u [u] 音。注意 o [o] 比 i [i] 和 u [u] 都要发得重些、长些。

When pronouncing iou [iou], the tongue position and mouth shape naturally slide from those of i [i] to those of o [o], and reach the position of u [u] finally. Note that o [o] is pronounced heavier and longer than both i [i] and u [u].

uei [uei]：先发 u [u] 的音，然后滑向发 e [e] 音，最后转到发 i [i] 音。注意这里的 e 发 [e]，并且比 u [u] 和 i [i] 都要发得重些、长些。

When pronouncing uei [uei], the tongue position and mouth shape naturally slide from those of u [u] to those of e [e], and reach the position of i [i] finally. Note that e is pronounced [e], and it is pronounced heavier and longer than both u [u] and i [i].

iao [iau]：先发 i [i] 的音，然后滑向发 a [ɑ] 音，最后转到发 o [u] 音。注

意这里的 ɑ 发 [ɑ]，并且比 i [i] 和 o [u] 都要发得重些、长些。

When pronouncing iɑo [iɑu], the tongue position and mouth shape naturally slide from those of i [i] to those of ɑ [ɑ], and reach the position of o [u] finally. Note that ɑ is pronounced [ɑ], and it is pronounced heavier and longer than both i [i] and o [u].

uɑi [uai]：先发 u [u] 音，然后滑向发 ɑ [a] 音，最后转到发 i [i] 音。注意这里的 ɑ 发 [a]，并且比 u [u] 和 i [i] 都要发得重些、长些。

When pronouncing uɑi [uai], the tongue position and mouth shape naturally slide from those of u [u] to those of ɑ [a], and reach the position of i [i] finally. Note that ɑ is pronounced [a], and it is pronounced heavier and longer than both u [u] and i [i].

ɑn [an]：先发 ɑ [a] 音，然后转向发 n [n] 音。注意这里的 ɑ 发 [a]。

When pronouncing ɑn [an], the tongue position and mouth shape naturally slide from those of ɑ [a] to those of n [n]. Note the ɑ here is pronounced as [a].

en [ən]：先发 e [ə] 音，然后转向发 n [n] 的音。注意这里的 e 发 [ə]。

When pronouncing en [ən], the tongue position and mouth shape naturally slide from those of e [ə] to those of n [n]. Note the e here is pronounced as [ə].

in [in]：先发 i [i] 音，然后转向发 n [n] 音。

When pronouncing in [in], the tongue position and mouth shape naturally slide from those of i [i] to those of n [n].

uen [uən]：先发 u [u] 音，然后滑向发 e [ə] 音，最后转向发 n [n] 音。注意这里的 e 发 [ə]。

When pronouncing uen [uən], the tongue position and mouth shape naturally slide from those of u [u] to those of e [ə], and reach the position of n [n] finally. Note the e here is pronounced as [ə].

ün [yn]：先发 ü [y] 音，然后转向发 n [n] 音。

When pronouncing ün [yn], the tongue position and mouth shape naturally slide from those of ü [y] to those of n [n].

ian [iɛn]：先发 i [i] 音，然后滑向发 a [ɛ] 音，最后转到发 n [n] 音。注意这里的 a 发 [ɛ]。

When pronouncing ian [iɛn], the tongue position and mouth shape naturally slide from those of i [i] to those of a [ɛ], and reach the position of n [n] finally. Note the a here is pronounced as [ɛ].

uan [uan]：先发 u [u] 音，然后滑向发 a [a] 音，最后转到发 n [n] 音。注意这里的 a 发 [a]。

When pronouncing uan [uan], the tongue position and mouth shape naturally slide from those of u [u] to those of a [a], and reach the position of n [n] finally. Note the a here is pronounced as [a].

üan [yan]：先发 ü [y] 音，然后滑向发 a [a] 音，最后转到发 n [n] 音。注意这里的 a 发 [a]。

When pronouncing üan [yan], the tongue position and mouth shape naturally slide from those of ü [y] to those of a [a], and reach the position of n [n] finally. Note the a here is pronounced as [a].

ang [ɑŋ]：先发 a [ɑ] 音，然后转向发 ng [ŋ] 音。注意这里的 a 发 [ɑ]。

When pronouncing ang [ɑŋ], the tongue position and mouth shape naturally slide from those of a [ɑ] to those of ng [ŋ]. Note the a here is pronounced as [ɑ].

eng [əŋ]：先发 e [ə] 音，然后转向发 ng [ŋ] 音。注意这里的 e 发 [ə]。

When pronouncing eng [əŋ], the tongue position and mouth shape naturally slide from those of e [ə] to those of ng [ŋ]. Note the e here is pronounced as [ə].

ing [iŋ]：先发 i [i] 音，然后转向发 ng [ŋ] 音。

When pronouncing ing [iŋ], the tongue position and mouth shape naturally slide from those of i [i] to those of ng [ŋ].

ong [uŋ]：先发 o [u] 音，然后转向发 ng [ŋ] 音。注意这里的 o 发 [u]。

When pronouncing ong [uŋ], the tongue position and mouth shape naturally slide from those of o [u] to those of ng [ŋ]. Note the o here is pronounced as [u].

iang [iaŋ]：先发 i [i]，然后滑向发 a [ɑ]，最后转到发 ng [ŋ] 音。注意这里的 a 发 [ɑ]。

When pronouncing iang [iaŋ], the tongue position and mouth shape naturally slide from those of i [i] to those of a [ɑ], and reach the position of ng [ŋ] finally. Note the a here is pronounced as [ɑ].

uang [uaŋ]：先发 u [u] 音，然后滑向发 a [ɑ] 音，最后转到发 ng [ŋ] 音。注意这里的 a 发 [ɑ]。

When pronouncing uang [uaŋ], the tongue position and mouth shape naturally slide from those of u [u] to those of a [ɑ], and reach the position of ng [ŋ] finally. Note the a here is pronounced as [ɑ].

ueng [uəŋ]：先发 u [u] 音，然后滑向发 e [ə] 音，最后转到发 ng [ŋ] 音。注意这里的 e 发 [ə]。

When pronouncing ueng [uəŋ], the tongue position and mouth shape naturally slide from those of u [u] to those of e [ə], and reach the position of ng [ŋ] finally. Note the e here is pronounced as [ə].

iong [yŋ]：先受协同发音作用的影响，将 i 和 o 协同发成 [y] 音，然后转向发 ng [ŋ] 音。注意这里的 i 和 o 协同发成 [y] 音。

When pronouncing iong [yŋ], affected by the coarticulation, i and o are co-articulately pronounced as [y], and pronounced as ng [ŋ] finally. Note the i and o here are pronounced as [y] due to the coarticulation.

三、声调　Tones

汉语普通话共有 4 个声调。各个声调的发音特点如下：

There are four tones in Mandarin Chinese. The pronunciation characteristics of each tone are as follows:

第一声：调形为高平调，调值为 [55]。

The first tone: The contour is high flat, and the tone pitch is [55].

第二声：调形为高升调，调值 [35]。

The second tone: The contour is high-rise, and the tone pitch is [35].

第三声：调形为降升调，调值为 [214]。

The third tone: The contour is fall-rise, and the tone pitch is [214].

第四声：调形为全降调，调值为 [51]。

The fourth tone: The contour is full-drop, and the tone pitch is [51].

汉语普通话 4 个声调的发音特点如图 1 所示。

The pronunciation characteristics of the four tones of Mandarin Chinese are summarized as shown in Figure 1.

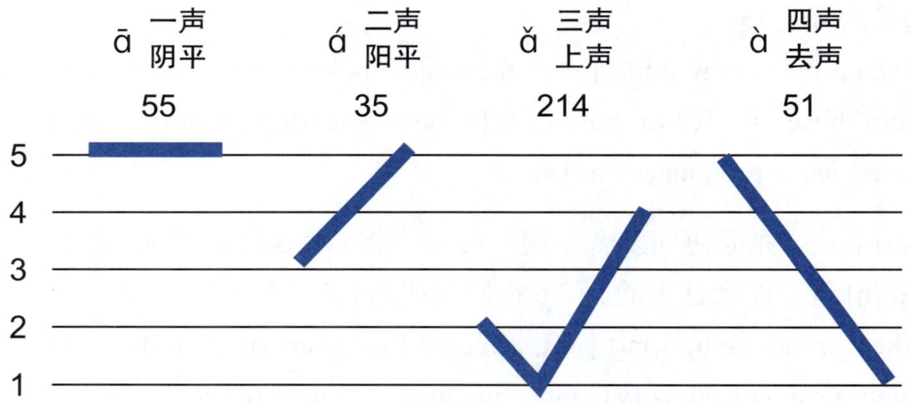

图 1　汉语普通话 4 个声调的发音特点示意图

四、句调　Intonation

句调就是整个句子音高升降的变化。汉语的句调主要表现为升调、降调、平调、曲调四种。

Intonation is the change in pitch of the entire sentence. The intonation of Chinese mainly comes in four types: declining, rising, flat, and tortuous.

1. 升调 Rising intonation

（1）你在干什么？↗（疑问）

（2）他真的走了？↗（惊异）

（3）你难道不知道？↗（反问）

2. 降调 Declining intonation

（1）请注意！↘（告诫）

（2）不要说话。↘（禁止）

（3）老师的课上得好！↘（感叹）

3. 平调 Flat intonation

（1）她是老师。（叙述，一般介绍）

（2）你自己决定吧。（冷淡）

（3）这是书。（叙述，一般介绍）

4. 曲调 Tortuous intonation

（1）你来得好早↘，现在还不到十二点！↗（讽刺）

（2）他↗厉害着↘呢。（意在话外）

（3）她↗还是↘老师？↗（意在话外）

交际项目一

见面问候

第一课
Lesson 1

Nǐ hǎo
你好

重点提示

- **交际功能：** 生人之间见面和问候。
- **主要生词：** 你、我、是。
- **主要语言点：** 人称代词“你”“我”，介绍姓名的“是”字句。
- **文化小常识：** 中国人的姓名。

一 看图讨论 Look at the picture and discuss

1. 他们在做什么？ What are they doing?
2. 他们会说什么呢？ What might they say?

二 课 文 Text

听录音回答问题 Listen to the recording and answer the following questions.

1. 这两个人的名字是什么？ What are the names of these two people?
2. 他们是怎么样介绍自己名字的？ How did they introduce their names?

Nǐ hǎo
你 好 1-1

Lǐ Ānpíng: Nǐ hǎo!
李安平：你 好！

Mǎ Wén: Nǐ hǎo!
马 文：你 好！

Lǐ Ānpíng: Wǒ shì Lǐ Ānpíng.
李安平：我 是 李 安 平。

Mǎ Wén: Wǒ shì Mǎ Wén.
马 文：我 是 马 文。

三 生 词 New words 1-2

1.	你好		nǐ hǎo	hello, hi
	你	代词	nǐ	you
	好	形容词	hǎo	fine, good
2.	我	代词	wǒ	I, me
3.	是	动词	shì	is, am, are
4.	李安平	专有名词	Lǐ Ānpíng	Li Anping, a person's name
5.	马文	专有名词	Mǎ Wén	Ma Wen, a person's name

四 主要语言点 Main language points

1 你好！

“你”是单数第二人称代词，在交际过程中，用来指代听话人。

“你” is a singular second person pronoun, which is used to refer to the listener in the communication process.

“你好”是与不认识的人第一次见面时打招呼的用语，任何时间都可以使用。对方也通常会用“你好”进行回复。

“你好” is a form of greeting used to greet someone you meet for the first time. It can be used at any time of a day. The response is usually also “你好”.

视频：1.1 你好（1）！

2 我是李安平。

“我”是单数第一人称代词，在交际过程中，用来指代说话人自己。

“我” is a singular first person pronoun, which is used to refer to the speaker himself in the communication process.

整个句子是一个用来介绍某人姓名的“是”字句。基本句式为“A 是 B”。其中，“A”可以是“我、他”等第一、第三人称代词；“B”可以是完整的姓名，也可以是姓加上职业等。例如：

This is a sentence with “是” used to introduce someone’s name. The basic sentence pattern is: “A是 B”. In the sentence, “A” can be a first or third personal pronoun, such as “我” and “他”; “B” can be a full name, or one’s surname plus occupation, etc. For example:

（1）他（tā）是马文。

（2）我是李老师（lǎoshī）。

视频：1.2 我是……

五 文化小常识 General knowledge of culture

中国人的姓名

中国人的姓名由姓和名两个部分组成，姓在前，名在后。中国人的姓多数是一个汉字，如“王、李”等；少数是两个汉字，如“司马、上官”等。中国人的名有的由两个汉字组成，如“李安平”中的“安平”；有的只有一个汉字，如“马文”中的“文”。

Chinese People's Names

A Chinese name is composed of two parts: the family name and the given name. The order of the two parts is: the family name comes before the given name. Most Chinese family names are monosyllabic, such as “王” and “李”. A few Chinese surnames are disyllabic, such as “司马”, “上官”, etc. Some Chinese given names are composed of two characters, such as “安平” in “李安平”; some are composed of only one character, such as “文” in “马文”.

六 练习与实践 Exercises and practice

1 听录音，选择你听到的声母，然后跟读三遍。 1-3

Listen to the recording and choose the initial you hear, then read the Pinyin three times after the recording.

(1) n / m / l } ǐ　　(2) k / g / h } ǎo　　(3) sh / s / c } ì

2 听录音，选择你听到的音，然后朗读下面的拼音。 1-4

Listen to the recording and choose the pronunciation you hear, then read the following Pinyin aloud.

(1) lǐ 李 — nǐ 你　　(2) hǎo 好 — lǎo 老　　(3) shí 十 — shì 是

(4) wǒ 我 — zuǒ 左　　(5) wán 玩 — wáng 王　　(5) wén 文 — wèn 问

3 看图选择词语，注意人物的手势。

Look at the pictures and choose the words, paying attention to their gestures.

我　　你

(1) ____________________

(2) ____________________

4 找出姓和名。

Find the family names and the given names.

王 文 平

（1）姓：_____ 名：_____

李丽

（2）姓：_____ 名：_____

张山

（3）姓：_____ 名：_____

江河

（4）姓：_____ 名：_____

司 马 光

（5）姓：_____ 名：_____

刘 一 民

（6）姓：_____ 名：_____

5 写出自己的中文姓名，并和自己第一语言的姓名比较一下儿，看看有什么不同。

Write down your Chinese name and compare it with your first language name to see the difference.

__________ __________

6 写出汉语老师的中文姓名，并和自己国家老师的姓名比较一下儿，看看有什么不同。

Write down the Chinese name of your Chinese teacher and compare it with the name of a teacher in your own country to see the difference.

__________ __________

7 替换练习。
Substitution drills

我是<u>马文</u>。	李安平 江山（Jiāng Shān） 王云平（Wáng Yúnpíng）

8 看图完成下面的对话，然后和同学一起演示一下儿对话的内容。
Look at the picture and complete the following dialogue, then act it out with your classmates.

A：你好！

B：________________！

A：我是________________。

B：我________________。

9 看视频，先回答问题，然后和同学一起表演视频的内容。

Watch the video and answer the questions. Then act out the video with your classmates.

（1）女生的名字是什么？

（2）男生的名字是什么？

视频：1.3 你好（2）！

10 汉字练习：看汉字笔画笔顺动态图，并跟着书写。

Practice Chinese characters: Look at the animated illustrations of the strokes and the order of strokes of the following characters, and then write them down.

nǐ
你

hǎo
好

wǒ
我

shì
是

第一课 汉字笔画笔顺动态图

第二课
Lesson 2

Wáng lǎoshī hǎo
王老师好

重点提示

- **交际功能：**一般熟人之间见面和问候。
- **主要生词：**老师、你们、早上。
- **主要语言点：**社会称呼语，表示复数的“们”。
- **文化小常识：**熟人见面时的汉语问候语。

一 看图讨论 Look at the picture and discuss

1. 他们在做什么？ What are they doing?
2. 他们会说什么呢？ What might they say?

二 课文 Text

听录音回答问题 Listen to the recording and answer the following questions.

1. 马文说了什么？ What did Ma Wen say?
2. 李安平说了什么？ What did Li Anping say?
3. 王老师说了什么？ What did Mr. Wang say?

Wáng lǎoshī hǎo
王 老师好 2-1

Mǎ Wén: Wáng lǎoshī hǎo!
马 文：王 老师 好！

Wáng lǎoshī: Nǐmen hǎo!
王老师：你们 好！

Lǐ Ānpíng: Wáng lǎoshī, zǎoshang hǎo!
李安平：王 老师，早上 好！

Wáng lǎoshī: Zǎoshang hǎo!
王老师：早上 好！

三 生词 New words 2-2

1.	王老师		Wáng lǎoshī	Mr./Ms. Wang
	老师	名词	lǎoshī	teacher

2.	你们	代词	nǐmen	you (*plural*)
	们	后缀	men	*a suffix used to indicate the plural*
3.	早上	名词	zǎoshang	morning

四 主要语言点 Main language points

1 王老师好！

"王老师"是最常用的汉语社会称呼语之一，它的一般构成方式为"姓+职业、职务/职称等"，如"王老师""李主任"等。

"王老师" is one of the most commonly used forms of address in Chinese society, which is generally composed of a surname plus an occupation / official rank / professional title, etc. For example,"王老师", "李主任", etc.

这是与熟人见面打招呼时的常用句之一。它由"王老师"等称呼语后面加上"好"构成，也可以由人名后面加上"好"构成。例如：

This is a sentence commonly used to greet an acquaintance. It is formed by adding "好" after a form of address such as "王老师" or after a person's name. For example:

（1）李主任（zhǔrèn）好！

（2）马文好！

视频：2.1 王老师好！

2 你们好！

“们”表示复数。它可以加在“你、我”等人称代词后面表示复数，也可以加在“老师、同学”等指人的名词后面表示复数。例如：

“们” indicates the plural. It can be used either after personal pronouns such as “你” and “我”, or after nouns referring to people such as “老师” and “同学” to indicate the plural. For example:

（1）我们是学生（xuéshēng）。

（2）老师们好！

（3）同学（tóngxué）们好！

视频：2.1 王老师好！

3 王老师，早上好！

“早上好”也是和熟人见面打招呼时的常用句。这种句子由“早上、中午、下午”等表示时间的名词后面加“好”构成。例如：

“早上好” is also a commonly used sentence to greet an acquaintance. It consists of a noun indicating time such as “早上”, “中午” or “下午” followed by “好”. For example:

（1）中午（zhōngwǔ）好！

（2）马文下午（xiàwǔ）好！

视频：2.2 早上好！

五 文化小常识 General knowledge of culture

熟人见面时的汉语问候语

中国人与比较熟的人见面时，如果这个人有比较好的职业、职务或职称时，人们常常用"姓＋职业（职务、职称）等称呼语＋好"来打招呼，例如"王老师好""马校长好"等；也常用"早上（中午、下午）＋好"来打招呼，例如"早上好""下午好"等。不过，前一种问候语比后一种显得更加正式一些。

Greeting Acquaintances in Chinese

When Chinese people greet an acquaintance, they often address the acquaintance in the form of "family name + occupation, official rank or professional title + 好" if the acquaintance has a decent occupation, official rank or professional title. For example, "王老师好", "马校长好" and so on. They also often address an acquaintance in the form of "早上 (中午, 下午) + 好". For example, "早上好", "下午好" and so on. However, the former is more formal than the latter.

六 练习与实践 Exercises and practice

1 听录音，选择你听到的声母，然后跟读三遍。2-3
Listen to the recording and choose the initial you hear, then read the Pinyin three times after the recording.

（1）n / m / l } ǎo
（2）zh / c / z } ǎo
（3）zh / ch / sh } ī

2 听录音，选择你听到的音，然后朗读下面的拼音。2-4
Listen to the recording and choose the pronunciation you hear, then read the following Pinyin aloud.

（1）您 nín — 你 nǐ
（2）好 hǎo — 老 lǎo
（3）早 zǎo — 老 lǎo
（4）们 men — 文 wén
（5）忙 máng — 王 wáng
（6）是 shì — 师 shī

3 替换练习。
Substitution drills

（1）你们
- 我
- 同学
- 朋友（péngyou）

（2）王老师好！
- 李老师
- 马老师
- 你们

（3）早上好！

中午
下午
晚上（wǎnshang）

4 看图完成下面的对话，然后和同学一起演示一下儿对话的内容。
Look at the picture and complete the following dialogue, then act it out with your classmates.

男　生：__________好！

王老师：__________！

女　生：王老师，__________好！

王老师：__________！

5 看视频，先回答问题，然后和同学一起表演视频的内容。
Watch the video and answer the questions. Then act out the video with your classmates.

（1）男生说了什么？

（2）王老师说了什么？

视频：2.1 王老师好！

6 和同学表演一下儿早上在校园里见面时的对话，注意用上下面的词语。
Act out the dialogue with your classmates whom you meet on campus in the morning. Use the following words.

你　　你们　　你们好　　早上好

7 汉字练习：看汉字笔画笔顺动态图，并跟着书写。
Practice Chinese characters: Look at the animated illustrations of the strokes and the order of strokes of the following characters, and then write them down.

wáng
王

lǎo
老

shī
师

men
们

zǎo
早

shang
上

第二课　汉字笔画笔顺动态图

第三课
Lesson 3

Zuìjìn hǎo ma
最近好吗

重点提示

- **交际功能**：很熟的人之间见面和问候。
- **主要生词**：最近、吗、很、也。
- **主要语言点**：疑问语气词“吗”，副词“很”“也”。
- **文化小常识**：老熟人见面时的汉语问候语。

一 看图讨论 Look at the picture and discuss

1. 他们在做什么？ What are they doing?
2. 他们会说什么呢？ What might they say?

二 课 文 Text

听录音回答问题 Listen to the recording and answer the following questions.

1. 马文说了什么？ What did Ma Wen say?
2. 李安平说了什么？ What did Li Anping say?

Zuìjìn hǎo ma
最近好吗 3-1

Mǎ Wén: Zuìjìn hǎo ma?
马 文：最近好吗？

Lǐ Ānpíng: Hěn hǎo. Nǐ hǎo ma?
李安平：很好。你好吗？

Mǎ Wén: Wǒ yě hěn hǎo.
马 文：我也很好。

三 生 词 New words 3-2

1.	最近	名词	zuìjìn	recently
2.	吗	助词	ma	*a particle used at the end of a yes/no question*
3.	很	副词	hěn	very
4.	也	副词	yě	also

四 主要语言点 Main language points

1 最近好吗？

“吗”是一个疑问语气助词，加在陈述句的末尾，用来表示疑问。例如：

“吗” is an interrogative particle added at the end of a declarative sentence to indicate a question. For example:

（1）你好！ + 吗 → 你好吗？

（2）他是老师。+ 吗 → 他是老师吗？

视频：3.1 最近好吗？

2 很好！

“很 + 形容词”表示程度高。例如：

“很 + adjective” indicates a high degree. For example:

（1）我很好！

（2）他们都（dōu）很好。

视频：3.1 最近好吗？

3 我也很好！

这个句子中的“也”表示类同，一般放在动词或形容词前面。当动词或形容词前面有副词“很”时，“也”要放在“很”的前面，构成“也 + 很 + 动词 / 形容词”的格式。例如：

"也" in this sentence is used to indicate similarity. It is usually used before a verb or an adjective. When the verb/adjective is preceded by the adverb "很", "也" is used before "很" to form the pattern "也 + 很 + verb/adjective". For example:

（1）你也是老师吗？
（2）我很好，老师也很好。

视频： 3.1 最近好吗？

五 文化小常识 General knowledge of culture

老熟人见面时的汉语问候语

中国人跟很熟的人见面时，如果彼此的年龄、身份相近，就会询问对方一些学习、生活等方面的情况，如"最近好吗""身体怎么样""学习怎么样"等。他们问这些问题的主要目的是表示与对方的亲近和友好。

Chinese Greetings Between Old Acquaintances

When Chinese people who are very familiar with each other meet, if they are similar in age and status, they might inquire about each other's study and life. For example, "最近好吗？", "身体怎么样？", "学习怎么样？", etc. The main purpose of asking these questions is to express their closeness and friendship with the other person.

六 练习与实践 Exercises and practice

1 听录音，选择你听到的韵母和声调，然后跟读三遍。3-3
Listen to the recording and choose the final and tone you hear, then read the Pinyin three times after the recording.

（1）z { uì / ì / è

（2）j { ìng / ūn / ìn

（3）h { ěn / ěng / ǎn

2 听录音，选择你听到的音，然后朗读下面的拼音。3-4
Listen to the recording and choose the pronunciation you hear, then read the following Pinyin aloud.

（1）最 zuì — 嘴 zuǐ
（2）号 hào — 好 hǎo
（3）亲 qīn — 近 jìn
（4）吗 ma — 马 mǎ
（5）肯 kěn — 很 hěn
（6）也 yě — 页 yè

3 朗读下面的句子，注意语气和语调。
Read the following sentences aloud, paying attention to the tone and intonation.

（1）最近好吗？
（2）很好！你好吗？
（3）我也很好！

4 排列词语成句子。
Arrange the words into sentences.

（1）吗　　好　　最近

____？

(2) 好 吗 你

______________________________?

(3) 很 好 我

______________________________。

(4) 也 我 很 也

______________________________。

5 看图完成下面的对话，然后和同学一起演示一下儿对话的内容。
Look at the picture and complete the following dialogue, then act it out with your classmates.

A：最近好________？

B：________好！你好________？

A：我________好！

6 看视频，先回答问题，然后和同学一起表演视频的内容。

Watch the video and answer the questions. Then act out the video with your classmates.

（1）男生问了什么？

（2）女生问了什么？

视频：3.1 最近好吗？

7 汉字练习：看汉字笔画笔顺动态图，并跟着书写。

Practice Chinese characters: Look at the animated illustrations of the strokes and the order of strokes of the following characters, and then write them down.

zuì
最

jìn
近

ma
吗

hěn
很

yě
也

第三课　汉字笔画笔顺动态图

交际项目二

咨询信息

第四课 Lesson 4

Tā shì shéi
他是谁

重点提示

- **交际功能：**询问相关的人。
- **主要生词：**他、谁、的、她、爸爸、妈妈。
- **主要语言点：**人称代词"他""她"，疑问代词"谁"，结构助词"的"。
- **文化小常识：**汉语中的亲属称谓。

一 看图讨论 Look at the picture and discuss

1. 他们在做什么？ What are they doing?
2. 他们在说什么呢？ What are they talking about?

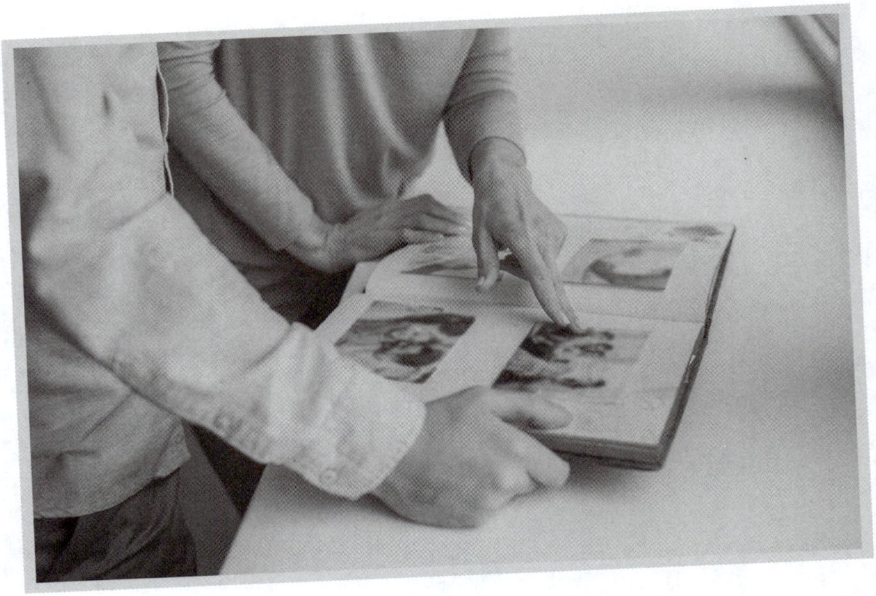

二 课 文 Text

听录音回答问题 Listen to the recording and answer the following questions.

1. 马文问了什么？ What did Ma Wen ask?
2. 李安平回答了什么？ What did Li Anping answer?

Tā shì shéi
他 是 谁 4-1

Mǎ Wén: Tā shì shéi?
马 文：他 是 谁？

Lǐ Ānpíng: Tā shì wǒ de bàba.
李安平：他 是 我 的 爸爸。

Mǎ Wén: Tā shì shéi?
马 文：她 是 谁？

Lǐ Ānpíng: Tā shì wǒ de māma.
李安平：她 是 我 的 妈妈。

三 生 词 New words 4-2

1.	他	代词	tā	he, him
2.	谁	代词	shéi	who
3.	的	助词	de	*used after an attribute to indicate possession*
4.	爸爸	名词	bàba	father, dad

5. 她	代词	tā	she, her
6. 妈妈	名词	māma	mother, mom

四 主要语言点 Main language points

1 他是谁?

“他”是指男性的单数第三人称代词。例如:

“他” is a singular third person pronoun that refers to a male person. For example:

(1) 他是我的爸爸。

(2) 他是我的老师。

(3) 他是老师吗?

“谁”是一个疑问代词,用于询问人,构成特指疑问句。例如:

“谁” is an interrogative pronoun used to ask about who someone is. It is used in a special interrogative sentence. For example:

(1) 你是谁?

(2) 谁是王老师?

(3) 他是谁的爸爸?

视频:4.1 他是谁?

2 他是我的爸爸。

结构助词“的”是定语的形式标志,要放在定语后边。名词或代词做定语,表示限定和修饰所有、所属的关系时，要加“的”。例如：

The structural particle “的” is the formal sign of the attribute, which should be placed after the attribute. When a noun/pronoun is used as an attribute to define, or show a possessive or subordinate relationship, “的” is used. For example:

（1）他是我的哥哥（gēge）。

（2）谁是我们的老师？

（3）他是我们的老师。

有时候，定语和中心语之间的结构助词“的”也可以不用。例如：

Sometimes, the structural particle “的” between the attribute and the head is omitted. For example:

（1）他是我哥哥。

（2）她是我妈妈。

（3）他爸爸是老师。

视频：4.1 他是谁？

3 她是谁？

“她”是指女性的单数第三人称代词。例如：

“她” is a singular third person pronoun that refers to a female person. For example:

（1）她是我的妈妈。

（2）她是你的姐姐（jiějie）吗？

（3）我是她的爸爸。

视频：4.2 她是谁？

五 文化小常识 General knowledge of culture

汉语中的亲属称谓

汉语中的亲属称谓比较多，有爷爷、奶奶、爸爸、妈妈、哥哥、姐姐、弟弟、妹妹、儿子、女儿、孙子、孙女、叔叔、姑姑、外公、外婆、表哥、表姐等。请注意，中国人对爸爸的兄弟和妈妈的兄弟的称呼是不同的，对爸爸的哥哥和爸爸的弟弟的称呼也是不同的。

Chinese Kinship Terms

There are many kinship terms in Chinese, including “爷爷”, “奶奶”, “爸爸”, “妈妈”, “哥哥”, “姐姐”, “弟弟”, “妹妹”, “儿子”, “女儿”, “孙子”, “孙女”, “叔叔”, “姑姑”, “外公”, “外婆”, “表哥”, “表姐”, etc. Please note that the appellations for one’s father’s brother and mother’s brother are different, so are the appellations for one’s father’s older brother and younger brother.

六 练习与实践 Exercises and practice

1 听录音，选择你听到的声母，然后跟读三遍。 4-3

Listen to the recording and choose the initial you hear, then read the Pinyin three times after the recording.

（1）d / t / l } ā　　（2）b / p / m } à　　（3）zh / ch / sh } éi

2 听录音，选择你听到的音，然后朗读下面的拼音。 4-4

Listen to the recording and choose the pronunciation you hear, then read the following Pinyin aloud.

（1）他 tā — 大 dà　　（2）打 dǎ — 她 tā　　（3）谁 shéi — 水 shuǐ

（4）怕 pà — 爸 bà　　（5）妈 mā — 吗 ma　　（6）得 dé — 的 de

3 朗读下面的句子，注意语调。

Read the following sentences aloud, paying attention to the intonation.

（1）他是谁？

（2）他是我的爸爸。

（3）她是我的妈妈。

4 看图完成下面的对话，然后和同学一起演示一下儿对话的内容。
Look at the picture and complete the following dialogues, then act out the dialogues with your classmates.

（1）A：他是________？

B：他是我________爸爸。

（2）A：________是________？

B：________是我妈妈。

（3）A：他是________？

B：________是我________爷爷（yéye）。

（4）A：________是________？

B：________是我________奶奶（nǎinai）。

5 替换练习。
Substitution drills

(1) 我的爸爸
- 你
- 他
- 她

(2) 他的妈妈
- 爸爸
- 弟弟（dìdi）
- 奶奶

6 拿着全家照，用汉语给同学们介绍一下儿自己的家人，注意用上下面的词语。
Take a photo of your whole family and introduce the members to your classmates in Chinese. Use the following words.

他　她　爸爸　妈妈　的　爷爷　奶奶

7 看视频，用汉语说说视频里介绍了谁。
Watch the video and tell who the video introduces.

视频：4.1 他是谁？

8 汉字练习：看汉字笔画笔顺动态图，并跟着书写。
Practice Chinese characters: Look at the animated illustrations of the strokes and the order of strokes of the following characters, and then write them down.

tā
他

shéi
谁

de
的

bà
爸

tā
她

mā
妈

第四课　汉字笔画笔顺动态图

第五课

Lesson 5

Zhè shì shénme

这是什么

重点提示

- **交际功能：** 询问相关的物品。
- **主要生词：** 这、什么、书、那、呢、手机。
- **主要语言点：** 指示代词“这”“那”，疑问代词“什么”，语气词“呢”。
- **文化小常识：** 手机的作用。

一 看图讨论 Look at the picture and discuss

1. 桌上有什么？ What's on the table?
2. 他们会说什么呢？ What might they say?

二 课文 Text

听录音回答问题 Listen to the recording and answer the following questions.

1. 马文问了什么？ What did Ma Wen ask?
2. 李安平回答了什么？ What did Li Anping answer?

Zhè shì shénme
这是什么 5–1

Mǎ Wén: Zhè shì shénme?
马　文：这是什么？

Lǐ Ānpíng: Zhè shì shū.
李安平：这是书。

Mǎ Wén: Nà shì shénme ne?
马　文：那是什么呢？

Lǐ Ānpíng: Nà shì shǒujī.
李安平：那是手机。

三 生词 New words 5–2

1.	这	代词	zhè	this
2.	什么	代词	shénme	what
3.	书	名词	shū	book
4.	那	代词	nà	that
5.	呢	助词	ne	*a particle used at the end of a question*
6.	手机	名词	shǒujī	mobile phone

四 主要语言点 Main language points

1 这是什么?

“这”指示比较近的人或事物。例如：

“这” indicates somebody or something nearby. For example:

（1）这是我的爸爸。

（2）这是笔（bǐ）。

用疑问代词“什么”提问，可构成汉语的特指疑问句，语序和陈述句相同。例如：

The interrogative pronoun “什么” is used to form a special interrogative sentence in Chinese. Its word order is the same as that of a declarative sentence. For example:

（1）这是什么书？

（2）这是什么笔？

视频：5.1 这是什么？

2 那是什么呢?

“那”指示比较远的人或事物。例如：

“那” indicates somebody or something that is far away. For example:

（1）那是我的妈妈。

（2）那是手机。

“呢”可以加在特指疑问句的句尾，起缓和语气的作用。例如：

“呢” can be used at the end of a special interrogative sentence to moderate the tone. For example:

（1）他是谁呢？

（2）这是什么呢？

（3）那是谁的书呢？

视频：5.2 那是什么呢？

五 文化小常识 General knowledge of culture

手机的作用

现在，手机成为人们日常生活中不可缺少的物品。人们除了用手机打电话外，还可以用它来发送语音、图片、视频等各种信息。另外，大家还可以用手机随时随地上网、听歌、看电影电视、扫码支付等。我们还可以用手机学习汉语。

The Role of Mobile Phones

Nowadays, mobile phones have become an indispensable item in people's daily life. In addition to making phone calls, people can also use a mobile phone to send voice messages, pictures, videos and other information. Besides these, we can also use mobile phones to surf the Internet, listen to songs, watch movies and TV, scan codes to pay, etc. anytime, anywhere. We can also use mobile phones to learn Chinese.

六 练习与实践 Exercises and practice

1 听录音，选择你听到的声调，然后跟读三遍。5-3
Listen to the recording and choose the tone you hear, then read the Pinyin three times after the recording.

(1) ˉ ˊ ˇ ˋ zhe　(2) ˉ ˊ ˇ ˋ na　(3) ˉ ˊ ˇ ˋ shen

(4) ˉ ˊ ˇ ˋ shou　(5) ˉ ˊ ˇ ˋ ji　(6) ˉ ˊ ˇ ˋ shu

2 听录音，选择你听到的音，然后朗读下面的拼音。5-4
Listen to the recording and choose the pronunciation you hear, then read the following Pinyin aloud.

(1) 舍 shè — 这 zhè　(2) 那 nà — 哪 nǎ　(3) 什 shén — 十 shí

(4) 手 shǒu — 少 shǎo　(5) 七 qī — 机 jī　(6) 出 chū — 书 shū

3 朗读下面的句子，注意语调。
Read the following sentences aloud, paying attention to the intonation.

(1) 这是什么？
(2) 那是什么呢？
(3) 那是手机。
(4) 那是书。
(5) 这是我的书。

4 选词填空。

Choose the words to fill in the blanks.

（1）________是什么？

A. 你　　　B. 这　　　C. 谁

（2）那是________。

A. 最近　　　B. 早上　　　C. 课本

5 排列词语成句子。

Arrange the words into sentences.

（1）什么　是　这

________________________？

（2）那　什么　是

________________________？

（3）什么　是　那　呢

________________________？

（4）这　书　我　的　是

________________________。

6 看图完成下面的对话，然后和同学一起演示一下儿对话的内容。
Look at the picture and complete the following dialogues, then act out the dialogues with your classmates.

（1）A：________是什么？
　　B：________是书。
　　A：________是________书？
　　B：________是我的书。

（2）A：________是什么？
　　B：________是手机。
　　A：________是________手机？
　　B：________是他的手机。

7 用“这”“那”给大家介绍一下儿教室里的东西。

Use the words “这” and “那” to introduce the things in the classroom.

8 看视频，先回答问题，然后和同学一起表演视频的内容。

Watch the video and answer the questions. Then act out the video with your classmates.

（1）男生说了什么？

（2）女生说了什么？

视频：5.3 这是书。

9 汉字练习：看汉字笔画笔顺动态图，并跟着书写。

Practice Chinese characters: Look at the animated illustrations of the strokes and the order of strokes of the following characters, and then write them down.

zhè
这

shén
什

me
么

shū
书

nà
那

ne
呢

shǒu
手

jī
机

第五课　汉字笔画笔顺动态图

第六课 Lesson 6

Nǐ yǒu Wáng lǎoshī de wēixìn ma

你有王老师的微信吗

重点提示

- **交际功能：** 询问别人的联系方式。
- **主要生词：** 有、微信、没有、那、邮箱、谢谢。
- **主要语言点：** 表示拥有的“有”及其否定形式“没有”，连词“那”。
- **文化小常识：** 中国人的常用联系方式。

一 看图讨论 Look at the picture and discuss

1. 下面的图片是什么？ What is in the picture below?
2. 如果你想得到别人的这些联系方式，会说什么呢？
   What will you say if you want to get the following contact information of others?

二 课 文 Text

听录音回答问题 Listen to the recording and answer the following questions.

1. 马文问了什么？ What did Ma Wen ask?
2. 李安平回答了什么？ What did Li Anping answer?

Nǐ yǒu Wáng lǎoshī de wēixìn ma
你有王老师的微信吗 6-1

Mǎ Wén: Nǐ yǒu Wáng lǎoshī de wēixìn ma?
马 文：你有王老师的微信吗？

Lǐ Ānpíng: Wǒ méiyǒu Wáng lǎoshī de wēixìn.
李安平：我没有王老师的微信。

Mǎ Wén: Nà nǐ yǒu Wáng lǎoshī de yóuxiāng ma?
马 文：那你有王老师的邮箱吗？

Lǐ Ānpíng: Wǒ yǒu Wáng lǎoshī de yóuxiāng.
李安平：我有王老师的邮箱。

Mǎ Wén: Xièxie!
马 文：谢谢！

三 生 词 New words 6-2

1. 有	动词	yǒu	have
2. 微信	名词	wēixìn	WeChat
3. 没有	动词	méiyǒu	not have
4. 那	连词	nà	that
5. 邮箱	名词	yóuxiāng	email address
6. 谢谢	动词	xièxie	thank you

四 主要语言点 Main language points

1 你有王老师的微信吗?

"有"可以用来表示领有，常用于"A+有+名词/名词短语"结构中。例如：

"有" is often used to indicate possession or ownership in the structure "A + 有 + noun / noun phrase". For example:

（1）我有书。

（2）他有手机。

（3）我有王老师的邮箱。

视频：6.1 你有王老师的微信吗？

2 我没有王老师的微信。

"没有"是"有"的否定式，常用于"A+没有+名词/名词短语"结构中。

例如：

"没有", the negative form of "有", is often used in the structure "A + 没有+ noun / noun phrase". For example:

（1）我没有书。

（2）他没有手机。

（3）我没有她的微信。

视频：6.1 你有王老师的微信吗？

3 那你有王老师的邮箱吗？

这个句子中的"那"是连词，用来承接上文，引进应该有的结果或是做出判断的分句，后面常有停顿。例如：

"那" in this sentence is a conjunction that serves to structurally introduce a clause which expresses the logical result or judgment. It is often followed by a pause. For example:

（1）A：你有哥哥吗？
B：我没有哥哥。
A：那你有弟弟吗？
B：我有弟弟。

（2）A：你有他的微信吗？
B：我没有他的微信。
A：那你有他的邮箱吗？
B：我有他的邮箱。

视频：6.1 你有王老师的微信吗？

五 文化小常识 General knowledge of culture

中国人的常用联系方式

现在，中国人的常用联系方式有打电话、发邮件、发微信等多种。其中，微信既可以用来发信息，也可以用来打电话，还可以用来视频聊天，非常方便。发送的信息既可以是文字，也可以是语音、图片、视频等。因此，微信成了中国人日常生活中最常用的联系方式之一。

Common Ways Chinese People Use to Contact Others

At present, Chinese people usually contact others by means of phone calls, emails, WeChat messages and so on. Among them, WeChat can be used to send messages, make phone calls and video chats, which is very convenient. The messages sent can be text messages, voice messages, pictures, videos, etc. Therefore, WeChat has become one of the most commonly used contact methods in Chinese people's daily life.

六 练习与实践 Exercises and practice

1 听录音，选择你听到的声调，然后跟读三遍。6-3
Listen to the recording and choose the tone you hear, then read the Pinyin three times after the recording.

(1) ˉ ˊ ˇ ˋ
you

(2) ˉ ˊ ˇ ˋ
you

(3) ˉ ˊ ˇ ˋ
mei

（4）ˉ ˊ ˇ ˋ
wei

（5）ˉ ˊ ˇ ˋ
xin

（6）ˉ ˊ ˇ ˋ
xie

2 听录音，选择你听到的音，然后朗读下面的拼音。6-4

Listen to the recording and choose the pronunciation you hear, then read the following Pinyin aloud.

（1）邮 yóu — 有 yǒu

（2）没 méi — 美 měi

（3）些 xiē — 谢 xiè

（4）美酒 měijiǔ — 没有 méiyǒu

（5）邮箱 yóuxiāng — 又想 yòu xiǎng

（6）微信 wēixìn — 没进 méi jìn

（7）写写 xiěxie — 谢谢 xièxie

3 朗读下面的句子，注意语调。

Read the following sentences aloud, paying attention to the intonation.

（1）我没有老师的微信。

（2）他有王老师的邮箱吗？

（3）她有王老师的微信。

（4）谢谢！

4 排列词语成句子。

Arrange the words into sentences.

（1）马文　的　你　邮箱　有　吗

______________________________？

（2）我　邮箱　的　李安平　没有

______________________________。

（3）有　的　老师　微信　你　吗　那

_______________________________?

（4）哥哥　的　微信　我　有

_______________________________。

5 看图完成下面的对话，然后和同学一起表演一下儿对话的内容。

Look at the picture and complete the following dialogue, then act it out with your classmates.

A：马文______哥哥吗？

B：马文______哥哥。

A：______马文______弟弟吗？

B：马文______弟弟。

6 替换练习：先替换画线的部分，然后和同学一起模仿对话。

Substitution drills: Replace the underlined parts first, then imitate the following dialogue with your classmates.

A：他有书吗？

B：他没有书。

A：那他有笔吗？

B：他有笔。

手机
微信
弟弟

电脑（diànnǎo）
邮箱
妹妹（mèimei）

7 说说你的书包里有什么，没有什么，注意用上下面的词语。

Talk about things that are in or not in your schoolbag. Use the following words.

有　没有　书　笔　手机

8 汉字练习：看汉字笔画笔顺动态图，并跟着书写。

Practice Chinese characters: Look at the animated illustrations of the strokes and the order of strokes of the following characters, and then write them down.

yǒu
有

wēi
微

xìn
信

méi
没

yóu
邮

xiāng
箱

xiè
谢

第六课　汉字笔画笔顺动态图

交际项目三

告　别

第七课

Lesson 7

Māma zàijiàn

妈妈再见

重点提示

- **交际功能：** 家人之间的日常告别。
- **主要生词：** 再见、路上、小心、晚上。
- **主要语言点：** 表示亲近用法的“小”，一般祈使句。
- **文化小常识：** 汉语的昵称。

一 看图讨论 Look at the picture and discuss

1. 她们在做什么？ What are they doing?
2. 她们会说什么呢？ What might they say?

二 课文 Text

听录音回答问题 Listen to the recording and answer the following questions.

1. 女儿说了什么？ What did the daughter say?
2. 妈妈说了什么？ What did the mother say?
3. 爸爸说了什么？ What did the father say?

Māma zàijiàn
妈妈 再见 7-1

nǚ'ér: Māma, zàijiàn!
女儿：妈妈，再见！

māma: Xiǎo Píng zàijiàn! Lùshang xiǎoxīn!
妈妈：小 平 再见！路上 小心！

nǚ'ér: Bàba, zàijiàn!
女儿：爸爸，再见！

bàba: Wǎnshang jiàn!
爸爸：晚上 见！

三 生词 New words 7-2

1.	再见	动词	zàijiàn	goodbye, bye
2.	女儿	名词	nǚ'er	daughter
3.	小平	专有名词	Xiǎo Píng	a nickname
	小	前缀	xiǎo	little, small

4. 路上	名词	lùshang	on the road
路	名词	lù	road
上	名词	shang	*used after a noun to indicate the scope of something*
5. 小心	形容词	xiǎoxīn	careful
6. 晚上	名词	wǎnshang	evening, night
7. 见	动词	jiàn	see

四 主要语言点 Main language points

1 妈妈，再见！

“再见”是一种常用的表达告别的方式。不管什么人、什么时候、在什么场合，与别人告别时都可以说“再见”。

常用的句式是“称呼语 + 再见”，也可以用“再见 + 称呼语”的形式。例如：

“再见” is a common way to say goodbye. You can use “再见” to bid farewell to anyone, at any time, on any occasion.

The commonly used sentence pattern is “form of address + 再见” or “再见 + form of address”. For example:

（1）A：再见，王老师！

B：同学们再见！

（2）再见，姐姐！

（3）爸爸，再见！

视频：7.1 再见！

2 小平再见！

在姓或者名前面加“小”，是对年轻人、小孩子的一种亲切的称呼，前者一般用于朋友、同事等熟人之间。例如：

“小” is used before a young person’s surname or given name to indicate affinity. It is usually used between friends, colleagues or acquaintances. For example:

（1）小王，谢谢你！
（2）再见，小华（Xiǎo Huá）。

视频：7.1 再见！

3 路上小心！

这是一句常用的表示关心的告别用语，多用于听话人即将出行的告别场合。

This is a common farewell expression to show concern. It is mostly used on farewell occasions when the listener is about to go out.

这是一个祈使句，主语一般是第一人称复数或第二人称，也可省略不出现，可用来表达建议、请求、要求等。例如：

This is an imperative sentence, whose subject is usually the first person plural or the second person. The subject can also be omitted. It can be used to express suggestions, requests, requirements, etc. For example:

（1）儿子（érzi）：妈妈，再见！
妈妈：再见！路上小心！
（2）学生：老师再见！
老师：小平再见！多（duō）联系（liánxì）！

视频：7.1 再见！

4 晚上见！

告别时，双方如果在比较短的时间内会再次见面，就可以用“时间 / 地点名词 + 见”这种告别用语。这种说明再次见面的具体时间、地点等的告别方式，略含说话人希望和对方见面的心理，从而表示一种友好、亲近的关系。例如：

"Time / place + 见" is a way of saying goodbye used by people who will meet again soon. Farewell expressions of this kind with the specific time and place of meeting again slightly indicate the speaker's hope to meet with the other party, thus expressing a friendly and close relationship. For example:

（1）中午见！

（2）下午见！

（3）学校（xuéxiào）见！

视频：7.2 晚上见！

五 文化小常识 General knowledge of culture

汉语的昵称

中国人在与朋友、同事等比较熟悉的人进行交际时，当对方是年轻人且年龄比自己小时，常在对方的姓或者名前面加上“小”来称呼对方，以表示和对方的亲昵关系。当对方年龄比较大且自己与其年龄相当时，则在对方的姓前面加上“老”（注意不能在名的前面加“老”）来称呼对方，也是表示和对方的亲昵关系。

Nicknames in Chinese

When communicating with a friend, colleague or acquaintance younger than themselves, Chinese people often add “小” before the other party’s surname or given name to express closeness with the other person. When the other party is older or of the same age as the speakers they often add “老” before the other party’s surname (be careful not to add “老” before the given name) to express closeness.

六 练习与实践 Exercises and practice

1 听录音，选择你听到的声母，然后跟读三遍。 7-3
Listen to the recording and choose the initial you hear, then read the Pinyin three times after the recording.

(1) z / c / s } ài　　(2) j / q / x } iàn　　(3) zh / ch / sh } àng

2 听录音，选择你听到的声调，然后跟读三遍。 7-4
Listen to the recording and choose the tone you hear, then read the Pinyin three times after the recording .

(1) ˉ ˊ ˇ ˋ xiao　　(2) ˉ ˊ ˇ ˋ lu　　(3) ˉ ˊ ˇ ˋ wan

3 听录音，选择你听到的音，然后朗读下面的拼音。 7-5
Listen to the recording and choose the pronunciation you hear, then read the following Pinyin aloud.

(1) 再 zài — 菜 cài　　(2) 小 xiǎo — 笑 xiào　　(3) 路 lù — 木 mù

(4) 晚 wǎn — 玩 wán　　(5) 山 shān — 上 shàng　　(6) 见 jiàn — 间 jiān

4 朗读下面的句子，注意语调。

Read the following sentences aloud, paying attention to the intonation.

（1）同学们再见！

（2）妈妈再见！

（3）路上小心！

（4）晚上见！

5 替换练习。

Substitution drills

（1）妈妈，再见！

爸爸
马文
王老师

（2）晚上见！

下午
明天（míngtiān）
明天早上

6 看图完成下面的对话，然后和同学一起演示一下儿对话的内容。

Look at the picture and complete the following dialogue, then act it out with your classmates.

爸爸：小华，__________！

李华：爸爸，__________！

爸爸：__________！

7 看视频，先回答问题，然后和同学一起表演视频的内容。

Watch the video and answer the questions. Then act out the video with your classmates.

（1）女儿说了什么？

（2）妈妈说了什么？

视频：7.1 再见！

8 汉字练习：看汉字笔画笔顺动态图，并跟着书写。

Practice Chinese characters: Look at the animated illustrations of the strokes and the order of strokes of the following characters, and then write them down.

zài
再

jiàn
见

nǚ
女

ér
儿

xiǎo
小

lù
路

xīn
心

wǎn
晚

第七课　汉字笔画笔顺动态图

第八课
Lesson 8

Duō liánxì
多联系

重点提示

- **交际功能：**一般朋友之间的告别。
- **主要生词：**请、留步、多、联系、慢走。
- **主要语言点：**“请”字开头的祈使句，表应答的“好的”。
- **文化小常识：**汉语的日常告别用语。

一 看图讨论 Look at the picture and discuss

1. 他们在做什么？ What are they doing?
2. 他们会说什么呢？ What might they say?

二 课 文 Text

听录音回答问题 Listen to the recording and answer the following questions.

1. 男的说了什么？ What did the man say?
2. 女的说了什么？ What did the woman say?

Duō liánxì
多联系 8–1

nán: Qǐng liúbù!
男：请留步！

nǚ: Nà duō liánxì!
女：那多联系！

nán: Hǎo de, zàijiàn!
男：好的，再见！

nǚ: Zàijiàn! Mànzǒu!
女：再见！慢走！

三 生 词 New words 8–2

1.	男	名词	nán	man
2.	请	动词	qǐng	please
3.	留步	动词	liúbù	(*a polite remark made to a host when a guest leaves*) don't bother to see me out

4. 女	名词	nǚ	woman
5. 多	形容词	duō	more
6. 联系	动词	liánxì	contact
7. 慢走	动词	mànzǒu	(at parting) goodbye, take care

四 主要语言点 Main language points

1 请留步!

这是一个用“请”字开头的祈使句，表示客气地让别人做某事，后面一般接表示动作行为的词。比如：

This is an imperative sentence beginning with “请”, which means to politely ask somebody to do something. It is usually followed by a word indicating action. For example:

（1）请进（jìn）！

（2）请坐（zuò）！

（3）请喝茶（hē chá）！

“请留步”是常用的告别用语，是主人送客时客人请主人不要再送而说的客套话。

“请留步” is a common expression for saying goodbye. It is a polite remark a guest makes to ask the host not to bother to see him out.

视频：8.1 请留步！

② 那多联系！

这是一句跟朋友、客人等告别时常说的客气话。

This is a polite remark often used when saying goodbye to a friend or guest.

视频：8.1 请留步！

③ 好的，再见！

"好的"表示答应或同意别人的请求、邀请或命令等。例如：

"好的" means to agree with or accept other people's request, invitation or order, etc. For example:

（1）A：多联系！

B：好的。

（2）A：这是你的书。

B：好的，谢谢！

视频：8.2 慢走！

④ 慢走！

这是送客时主人说的客套话，表示提醒对方路上注意安全。

This is a polite remark a host makes when seeing a guest out, reminding him to take care on the road.

视频：8.2 慢走！

五 文化小常识 General knowledge of culture

汉语的日常告别用语

在一般的社会交际中，中国人在与朋友、同事等告别时，除了说“再见”外，还常常说一些表示关心、提醒等的客套话，比如“路上小心”“多联系”“慢走”等。这些日常告别用语表达了说话人与对方的亲近和友好。

Daily Farewell Expressions in Chinese

In social communication, when Chinese people say goodbye to their friends or colleagues, besides “再见”, they often say some polite remarks to show their concern or remind others, such as “路上小心”, “多联系”, or “慢走”. These daily farewell expressions show the affinity and friendliness between the speaker and the other party.

六 练习与实践 Exercises and practice

1 听录音，选择你听到的韵母和声调，然后跟读三遍。8-3
Listen to the recording and choose the final and tone you hear, then read the Pinyin three times after the recording.

(1) q { ǐn / ěng / ǐng }

(2) l { ǒu / iú / ú }

(3) d { uō / ō / ōu }

2 听录音，选择你听到的声调，然后跟读三遍。8–4

Listen to the recording and choose the tone you hear, then read the Pinyin three times after the recording.

（1）ˉ ˊ ˇ ˋ lian　　（2）ˉ ˊ ˇ ˋ xi　　（3）ˉ ˊ ˇ ˋ zou

3 听录音，选择你听到的音，然后朗读下面的拼音。8–5

Listen to the recording and choose the pronunciation you hear, then read the following Pinyin aloud.

（1）请 qǐng — 醒 xǐng　　（2）六 liù — 留 liú　　（3）多 duō — 都 dōu

（4）系 xì — 气 qì　　（5）馒 mán — 慢 màn　　（6）走 zǒu — 左 zuǒ

（7）练习 liànxí — 联系 liánxì　　（8）慢走 mànzǒu — 馒头 mántou

4 朗读下面的句子，注意语调。

Read the following sentences aloud, paying attention to the intonation.

（1）老师，请慢走！

（2）请留步！

（3）那多联系！

5 排列词语成句子。

Arrange the words into sentences.

（1）留步　你　请

________________________________！

（2）联系　那　多

________________________________！

（3）再见　好　的

____!

6 替换练习。
Substitution drills

（1）请留步！	进 坐 喝茶
（2）那多联系。	锻炼（duànliàn） 看书 复习

7 看图完成下面的对话，然后和同学一起演示一下儿对话的内容。
Look at the picture and complete the following dialogue, then act it out with your classmates.

男：请＿＿＿＿＿＿＿！

女：那＿＿＿＿＿＿＿！

男：＿＿＿＿＿＿＿，再见！

女：再见！＿＿＿＿＿＿＿！

8 介绍一下儿中国朋友之间分别时说的话，注意用上下面的词语。
Introduce what Chinese people say when they part with their friends. Use the following words.

请　　留步　　多　　联系　　慢走

9 汉字练习：看汉字笔画笔顺动态图，并跟着书写。
Practice Chinese characters: Look at the animated illustrations of the strokes and the order of strokes of the following characters, and then write them down.

nán
男

qǐng
请

liú
留

bù
步

duō
多

lián
联

xì
系

màn
慢

zǒu
走

第八课 汉字笔画笔顺动态图

第九课
Lesson
9

Yílù píng'ān

一路平安

重点提示

- **交际功能：**与贵宾的庄重告别。
- **主要生词：**一路、平安、不客气、欢迎、去、国家。
- **主要语言点：**否定副词“不”，兼语句，祝福语“一路平安”。
- **文化小常识：**汉语庄重场合中的告别祝福语。

一 看图讨论 Look at the picture and discuss

1. 他们在做什么？ What are they doing?
2. 他们会说什么呢？ What might they say?

二 课文 Text

听录音回答问题 Listen to the recording and answer the following questions.

1. 男的说了什么？ What did the man say?
2. 女的说了什么？ What did the woman say?

Yílù píng'ān
一路平安 9-1

nán： Xièxie nǐmen!
男： 谢谢 你们！

nǚ： Bú kèqi!
女： 不 客气！

nán： Huānyíng nǐmen qù wǒmen guójiā. Zàijiàn!
男： 欢迎 你们去我们国家。再见！

nǚ： Xièxie! Zàijiàn! Yílù píng'ān!
女： 谢谢！ 再见！ 一路 平安！

三 生词 New words 9-2

1.	一路	名词	yílù	all the way, throughout the journey
2.	平安	形容词	píng'ān	safe and sound
3.	不客气		bú kèqi	you are welcome

4. 欢迎	动词	huānyíng	welcome
5. 去	动词	qù	go
6. 我们	代词	wǒmen	we, us
7. 国家	名词	guójiā	country

四 主要语言点 Main language points

1 不客气！

“不”是一个表示否定的副词，这里是“不必、不用”的意思。这是一句常用的回复别人感谢的客套话。例如：

“不” is an adverb indicating negation. Here it means “unnecessary” or “no need”. It is usually used as a remark in response to others' gratefulness. For example:

（1）学生：谢谢老师！

老师：不客气！

（2）乘客（chéngkè）：谢谢！

司机（sījī）：不客气！

视频：9.1 不客气！

2 欢迎你们去我们国家。

“欢迎你们去我们国家”是一个兼语句。这种句子的谓语由兼语短语构成，即前一个动词的宾语又是第二个动词的主语。句子的语序是：

（主语＋）动词$_1$＋兼语（宾语、主语）＋动词$_2$＋宾语

“欢迎你们去我们国家” is a pivotal sentence. The predicate of this kind of sentence contains a concurrent phrase, which is both the object of the first verb and the subject of the second verb. The word order of a pivotal sentence is:

(Subject +) Verb$_1$ + Pivotal structure (Object, Subject) + Verb$_2$ + Object

例如：

For example:

（1）请你喝茶！

（2）欢迎老师去我们国家！

（3）欢迎你去我家（jiā）！

视频：9.2 欢迎你们去我们国家！

3 一路平安！

“一路平安”是祝福别人旅途顺利、平安的祝福语。例如：

“一路平安” is used to wish somebody a smooth and safe journey. For example:

（1）祝你们一路平安！

（2）祝爸爸一路平安！

（3）祝老师一路平安！

视频：9.2 欢迎你们去我们国家！

五 文化小常识 General knowledge of culture

汉语庄重场合中的告别祝福语

在中国的一些庄重的社交场合中，在向主人正式告别时，客人常常要对主人说一些感谢的话，如“感谢热情接待”“感谢细心关照”等等，有时还会向主人发出邀请。主人常常对客人说一些祝福的话，如“一路平安”“旅途愉快”等等。

Solemn Farewell Wishes in Chinese

On some solemn social occasions in China, when bidding farewell to the host, the guest often expresses his gratitude to the host by saying “感谢热情接待”, “感谢细心关照”, etc., and sometimes he extends an invitation to the host. The host often expresses his good wishes to the guest by saying “一路平安”, “旅途愉快”, etc.

六 练习与实践 Exercises and practice

1 听录音，选择你听到的声母，然后跟读三遍。 9–3
Listen to the recording and choose the initial you hear, then read the Pinyin three times after the recording.

(1) j / q / x } ì　　(2) k / g / h } è　　(3) b / p / l } íng

2 听录音，选择你听到的声调，然后跟读三遍。 9–4

Listen to the recording and choose the tone you hear, then read the Pinyin three times after the recording.

（1）ˉ ˊ ˇ ˋ guo　　（2）ˉ ˊ ˇ ˋ ying　　（3）ˉ ˊ ˇ ˋ qu

3 听录音，选择你听到的音，然后朗读下面的拼音。 9–5

Listen to the recording and choose the pronunciation you hear, then read the following Pinyin aloud.

（1）祝 zhù — 主 zhǔ　　（2）您 nín — 你 nǐ　　（3）可 kě — 客 kè

（4）欢 huān — 换 huàn　　（5）迎 yíng — 应 yīng　　（6）去 qù — 取 qǔ

（7）我们 wǒmen — 五 门 wǔ mén　　（8）汉英 Hàn-Yīng — 欢迎 huānyíng

（9）过 江 guò jiāng — 国家 guójiā　　（10）平安 píng'ān — 饼干 bǐnggān

4 朗读下面的句子，注意语调。

Read the following sentences aloud, paying attention to the intonation.

（1）谢谢你们！

（2）一路平安！

（3）欢迎你们去我们国家！

（4）不客气！

5 替换练习。
Substitution drills

（1）谢谢<u>你们</u>！

你
妈妈
马文

（2）欢迎<u>你</u>去我们家！

您
小平
李老师

6 排列词语成句子。
Arrange the words into sentences.

（1）你们　谢谢

________________________________！

（2）平安　一路

________________________________！

（3）我们　去　你们　国家　欢迎

________________________________！

7 看图完成下面的对话，然后和同学一起演示一下儿对话的内容。
Look at the picture and complete the following dialogue, then act it out with your classmates.

A：谢谢你们！

B：________客气！

A：________你们________我们国家！

B：谢谢！________！

8 看视频，先回答问题，然后和同学一起表演视频的内容。

Watch the video and answer the questions. Then act out the video with your classmates.

（1）男的说了什么？

（2）女的说了什么？

视频：9.2 欢迎你们去我们国家！

9 汉字练习：看汉字笔画笔顺动态图，并跟着书写。

Practice Chinese characters: Look at the animated illustrations of the strokes and the order of strokes of the following characters, and then write them down.

yī
一

píng
平

ān
安

bù
不

kè
客

qi
气

huán
欢

yíng
迎

qù
去

guó
国

jiā
家

第九课　汉字笔画笔顺动态图

综合实践一

第十课

Lesson 10

Qǐngwèn nín guìxìng

请问您贵姓

重点提示

- **交际功能：** 礼貌地询问姓名。
- **主要生词：** 请问、您、贵姓、免、姓、叫。
- **主要语言点：** 第二人称尊称“您”，疑问句“请问……？”，用于介绍姓名的“叫”字句。
- **文化小常识：** 汉语中礼貌询问姓名和回答的方式。

一 看图讨论 Look at the picture and discuss

1. 他们在做什么？ What are they doing?
2. 他们会说什么呢？ What might they say?

二 课 文 Text

听录音回答问题 Listen to the recording and answer the following questions.

1. 王老师问了什么？ What did Mr. Wang ask?
2. 江山是怎么回答的？ How did Jiang Shan answer him?

Qǐngwèn nín guìxìng
请问 您 贵姓 10–1

Wáng lǎoshī: Nín hǎo!
王 老师：您 好！

Jiāng Shān: Nín hǎo!
江 山：您 好！

Wáng lǎoshī: Wǒ shì Wáng Yúnpíng. Qǐngwèn nín guìxìng?
王 老师：我 是 王 云平。请问 您 贵姓？

Jiāng Shān: Miǎn guì xìng Jiāng, jiào Jiāng Shān.
江 山：免 贵 姓 江，叫 江 山。

三 生 词 New words 10–2

1.	请问	动词	qǐngwèn	*an honorific expression used to ask the other party to answer a question*
	问	动词	wèn	ask

2.	您	代词	nín	you (*honorific*)
3.	贵姓	名词	guìxìng	*an honorific expression for asking the other party's family name*
4.	王云平	专有名词	Wáng Yúnpíng	Wang Yunping, a person's name
5.	免	动词	miǎn	don't have to...
6.	姓	动词	xìng	have as a surname
7.	叫	动词	jiào	call, be called
8.	江山	专有名词	Jiāng Shān	Jiang Shan, a person's name

四 主要语言点 Main language points

1 请问您贵姓？

“请问”用来客气地、礼貌地询问别人的某个问题或提出某项请求，一般用于句子的开头，后面接着要问的问题或请求的事项。

“请问” is a polite expression used to ask somebody a question or make a request. It is generally used at the beginning of a sentence, followed by a question or request.

“您”是第二人称代词“你”的敬称。对上了年纪的人、比自己年长的人或有身份和地位的人，在汉语普通话中都要用“您”来称呼对方。

“您” is a term of respect of the second person pronoun “你”. It is used to address the aged or people older than or superior to the speaker.

"贵姓"表示很礼貌、很客气地询问对方姓氏，常常和表示尊敬的人称代词"您"一起使用，构成"您贵姓"的格式。例如：

"贵姓" is a polite expression used to ask somebody's surname, which is often used together with the personal pronoun "您" to show respect, forming the structure "您贵姓". For example:

（1）请问您贵姓？

（2）请问您是王老师吗？

（3）马文，请问您有老师的邮箱吗？

视频：10.1 请问您贵姓？

2 免贵姓江。

"免"在这里是"不必、不用"的意思。"免贵姓……"一般用于回答"您贵姓"这个问题，后面紧接着介绍自己的姓。例如：

"免" means "unnecessary" or "need not". "免贵姓……" is usually used to answer the other party's question "您贵姓" and is followed by the person's own surname. For example:

（1）A：您贵姓？

B：免贵姓马。

（2）A：请问您贵姓？

B：免贵姓王。

视频：10.1 请问您贵姓？

3 叫江山。

这类句子中的“叫”用于介绍姓名，即“叫”的后面紧接着某人的姓名。基本句型是“A 叫 B”，相当于“A 的名字是 B”。例如：

“叫” in this kind of sentence is used to introduce one’s name, i.e., “叫” is followed by someone’s name. The basic sentence pattern is “A 叫 B”, which is equal to “A’s name is B”. For example:

（1）A：你叫什么？

B：我叫马文。

（2）A：她叫什么？

B：她叫李安平。

视频：10.1 请问您贵姓？

五 文化小常识 General knowledge of culture

汉语中礼貌询问姓名和回答的方式

在中国，人们在与不认识的人在正式场合初次见面时，特别是与比自己年长的人、有身份和地位的人初次见面时，如果想知道对方的姓氏，就会用“请问您贵姓”这种非常礼貌、非常客气的问句。在回答别人这一问题时，也会用“免贵姓……” 这种礼貌而客气的表达方式。

Polite Inquiries and Replies in Chinese

In China, when a person meets a stranger for the first time on formal occasions, especially when the person is older than himself, or higher in status, if he wants to know the person's surname, he will ask: "请问您贵姓？" This is a very polite question. In response to this question, the other person will politely answer: "免贵姓……".

六 练习与实践 Exercises and practice

1 听录音，选择你听到的声母，然后跟读三遍。 10–3
Listen to the recording and choose the initial you hear, then read the Pinyin three times after the recording .

（1）{j / q / x} ǐng　　（2）{g / k / h} uì　　（3）{s / ch / sh} ān

2 听录音，选择你听到的韵母和声调，然后跟读三遍。 10–4
Listen to the recording and choose the final and tone you hear, then read the Pinyin three times after the recording.

（1）n {í / ín / íng}　　（2）j {ià / ào / iào}　　（3）m {ǎn / ǎng / iǎn}

3 听录音，选择你听到的声调，然后跟读三遍。 10–5
Listen to the recording and choose the tone you hear, then read the Pinyin three times after the recording.

（1）ˉ ˊ ˇ ˋ mian　　（2）ˉ ˊ ˇ ˋ qing　　（3）ˉ ˊ ˇ ˋ nin

4 听录音，选择你听到的音，然后朗读下面的拼音。 10-6

Listen to the recording and choose the pronunciation you hear, then read the following Pinyin aloud.

qīng　qǐng （1）轻 — 请	wén　wèn （2）文 — 问	nín　nǐ （3）您 — 你
guì　huì （4）贵 — 会	xìng　xíng （5）姓 — 行	miǎn　nián （6）免 — 年
xiào　jiào （7）校 — 叫	jiāng　jiàn （8）江 — 见	shān　sān （9）山 — 三

5 朗读下面的句子，注意语调。

Read the following sentences aloud, paying attention to the intonation.

（1）请问您贵姓？

（2）免贵姓王。

（3）他叫什么？

（4）他叫江山。

6 排列词语成句子。

Arrange the words into sentences.

（1）是　王云平　我

________________________________。

（2）贵姓　请问　您

________________________________？

（3）姓　贵　李　免

________________________________。

（4）叫　马文　我

________________________________。

7 替换练习。

Substitution drills

(1) 请问<u>您贵姓</u>?

他是谁
这是什么
您有王老师的邮箱吗

(2) 我是<u>马文</u>，请问您贵姓?

王云平
江山
李安平

(3) 免贵姓<u>王</u>，叫<u>王云平</u>。

江　江山
李　李安平
马　马文

8 看图完成下面的对话，然后和同学一起演示一下儿对话的内容。

Look at the picture and complete the following dialogue, then act it out with your classmates.

A：您好！________您________姓？

B：________好！________姓李，________李安平。

9 看视频，先回答问题，然后和同学一起表演视频的内容。

Watch the video and answer the questions. Then act out the video with your classmates.

（1）男的问了什么？

（2）女的回答了什么？

视频：10.1 请问您贵姓？

10 介绍一下儿在中国的正式场合中人们见面的问候方式或者你自己的一次正式见面经历，注意用上下面的词语。

Introduce how people greet each other on formal occasions in China or one of your own experiences of meeting someone formally. Use the following words.

请问　　您　　贵姓　　免贵　　姓　　叫

11 汉字练习：看汉字笔画笔顺动态图，并跟着书写。

Practice Chinese characters: Look at the animated illustrations of the strokes and the order of strokes of the following characters, and then write them down.

wèn
问

nín
您

miǎn
免

guì
贵

xìng
姓

jiào
叫

第十课 汉字笔画笔顺动态图

第十一课
Lesson 11

Tā shì nǎ guó rén

他是哪国人

重点提示

- **交际功能：**谈论个人国籍等信息。
- **主要生词：**哪、国、不。
- **主要语言点：**疑问代词“哪”，副词“不”。
- **文化小常识：**世界与中国。

一 看图讨论 Look at the picture and discuss

1. 如果你想知道别人的国籍，该怎么问呢？
   If you want to know someone's nationality, what should you ask?
2. 如果我们告诉别人我们的国籍，该怎么说呢？
   What should we say if we want to tell others our nationality?

二 课文 Text

听录音回答问题 Listen to the recording and answer the following questions.

1. 马文问了什么？ What did Ma Wen ask?
2. 李安平是怎么回答他的？ How did Li Anping answer him?

Tā shì nǎ guó rén
他是哪国人 11-1

Lǐ Ānpíng: Tā shì nǎ guó rén ?
李 安平： 他是哪国人？

Mǎ Wén: Tā shì Měiguórén.
马 文： 他是美国人。

Lǐ Ānpíng: Nǐ yě shì Měiguórén ma ?
李 安平： 你也是美国人吗？

Mǎ Wén: Wǒ bú shì Měiguórén, wǒ shì Tàiguórén.
马 文： 我不是美国人，我是泰国人。

Lǐ Ānpíng: Xièxie!
李 安平： 谢谢！

Mǎ Wén: Bú kèqi!
马 文： 不客气！

三 生 词 New words 11-2

1.	哪	代词	nǎ	which
2.	国	名词	guó	country
3.	人	名词	rén	person, people
4.	不	副词	bù	not
5.	美国人	专有名词	Měiguórén	American (people)
	美国	专有名词	Měiguó	the United States
6.	泰国人	专有名词	Tàiguórén	Thai (people)
	泰国	专有名词	Tàiguó	Thailand

四 主要语言点 Main language points

1 他是哪国人?

用疑问代词“哪”提问的句子是汉语的特指疑问句，语序和原有的陈述句相同。例如：

A sentence using the interrogative pronoun “哪” is a special interrogative sentence in Chinese, whose word order is the same as that of a declarative sentence. For example:

（1）她是哪国人?

（2）马文是哪国人?

（3）你的同学是哪国人?

"国家名 + 人"是说明某人国籍（属于某一个国家）的常用表达格式。例如：

"Country name +人" is a common expression to introduce someone's nationality, that is, the country someone belongs to. For example:

（1）他是中国（Zhōngguó）人。

（2）马文是泰国人。

（3）他是马来西亚（Mǎláixīyà）人。

（4）李华是老挝（Lǎowō）人。

（5）王主任是印度尼西亚（Yìndùníxīyà）人。

视频：11.1 他是哪国人？

2 我不是美国人。

"不"是一个表示否定的副词。例如：

"不" is an adverb that indicates negation. For example:

（1）他不是泰国人。

（2）马文不是老师。

（3）这不是课本。

视频：11.1 他是哪国人？

五 文化小常识 General knowledge of culture

世界与中国

世界上共有七大洲，分别是亚洲、非洲、欧洲、大洋洲、北美洲、南美洲以及南极洲，共包括两百多个国家和地区。中国属于亚洲，位于北半球的亚洲东部。世界上有十四个国家的陆地与中国相邻，如越南、老挝、印度、俄罗斯等。同中国隔海相望的邻国有六个，分别是韩国、日本、菲律宾、文莱、马来西亚、印度尼西亚。

The World and China

There are seven continents in the world, namely Asia, Africa, Europe, Oceania, North America, South America and Antarctica, with a total of more than 200 countries and regions. China belongs to Asia and is located in the eastern part of Asia in the Northern Hemisphere. The land of 14 countries in the world is adjacent to China, including Vietnam, Laos, India, Russia and other countries. There are six neighboring countries across the sea from China, respectively including South Korea, Japan, the Philippines, Brunei, Malaysia and Indonesia.

六 练习与实践 Exercises and practice

1 听录音，选择你听到的韵母和声调，然后跟读三遍。 11-3
Listen to the recording and choose the final and tone you hear, then read the Pinyin three times after the recording.

(1) r { én / éng / án }　　(2) g { ú / ó / uó }　　(3) t { ài / ào / èi }

2 听录音，选择你听到的声调，然后跟读三遍。 11-4
Listen to the recording and choose the tone you hear, then read the Pinyin three times after the recording.

(1) ˉ ˊ ˇ ˋ na　　(2) ˉ ˊ ˇ ˋ bu　　(3) ˉ ˊ ˇ ˋ mei

3 听录音，选择你听到的音，然后朗读下面的拼音。 11-5
Listen to the recording and choose the pronunciation you hear, then read the following Pinyin aloud.

(1) nǎ 哪 — mǎ 马　　(2) sì 四 — shì 是　　(3) guó 国 — guò 过

(4) měi 美 — méi 没　　(5) zài 再 — tài 泰　　(6) yě 也 — xiě 写

(7) méi guò 没 过 — Měiguó 美国　　(8) Tàiguó 泰国 — dàiguò 带过

4 朗读下面的句子，注意语调和重音。

Read the following sentences aloud, paying attention to the intonation and stress.

（1）他是哪国人？

（2）他是美国人。

（3）你也是美国人吗？

（4）我不是美国人，我是泰国人。

5 排列词语成句子。

Arrange the words into sentences.

（1）人　国　是　她　哪

______________________________？

（2）你　吗　人　中国　是

______________________________？

（3）老师　中国　是　人

______________________________。

（4）是　也　美国　他　不　人

______________________________。

（5）是　人　不　马文　中国

______________________________。

6 替换练习：先替换画线的部分，然后和同学一起模仿对话。

Substitution drills: Replace the underlined parts first, then imitate the following dialogues with your classmates.

（1）A：她是哪国人？
　　B：她是美国人。

王老师　　中国
他　　马来西亚
马文　　泰国

（2）A：你也是美国人吗？
　　B：我不是美国人。

他
小王
李安平

7 看图完成下面的对话，然后和同学一起演示一下儿对话的内容。

Look at the picture and complete the following dialogue, then act it out with your classmates.

女：他是________国人？

男：他是________人。

女：你也是________人吗？

男：________是，我是________人。

8 用汉语介绍一下儿自己是哪国人，然后再介绍一下儿班上的同学分别是哪国人。

Use Chinese to introduce which country you are from, then introduce which countries the students in your class are from.

9 看视频，先回答问题，然后和同学一起表演视频的内容。

Watch the video and answer the questions. Then act out the video with your classmates.

（1）女生问了什么？

（2）男生回答了什么？

（3）男生是美国人吗？

视频：11.1 他是哪国人？

10 汉字练习：看汉字笔画笔顺动态图，并跟着书写。

Practice Chinese characters: Look at the animated illustrations of the strokes and the order of strokes of the following characters, and then write them down.

nǎ 哪

rén 人

měi 美

tài

泰

第十一课 汉字笔画笔顺动态图

第十二课 Lesson 12

Nàxiē shì shéi de xuéshēngzhèng ne
那些是谁的学生证呢

重点提示

- **交际功能：** 询问物品信息。
- **主要生词：** 那些、些、学生证、这些、课本、都、同学。
- **主要语言点：** 表示不定量的“些”，指示代词“这些”“那些”，副词“都”。
- **文化小常识：** 中国人的重要证件。

一 看图讨论 Look at the picture and discuss

1. 下面的图片是什么？ What is in the picture below?
2. 你有吗？它有什么作用呢？ Do you have it? What is it used for?

二 课 文 Text

听录音回答问题 Listen to the recording and answer the following questions.

1. 这些是什么？ What are these?
2. 那些是什么？ What are those?

Nàxiē shì shéi de xuéshēngzhèng ne
那些是谁的 学生证 呢 12-1

Mǎ Wén: Zhèxiē shì shénme?
马　文：这些是什么？

Lǐ Ānpíng: Zhèxiē shì kèběn.
李 安平：这些是课本。

Mǎ Wén: Nàxiē yě shì kèběn ma?
马　文：那些也是课本吗？

Lǐ Ānpíng: Bú shì, nàxiē dōu shì xuéshēngzhèng.
李 安平：不是，那些都是 学生证。

Mǎ Wén: Shì shéi de xuéshēngzhèng ne?
马　文：是谁的 学生证 呢？

Lǐ Ānpíng: Dōu shì tóngxuémen de xuéshēngzhèng.
李 安平：都是同学们的 学生证。

三 生词 New words 12-2

1.	那些	代词	nàxiē	those
	些	量词	xiē	some
2.	学生证	名词	xuéshēngzhèng	student ID
3.	这些	代词	zhèxiē	these
4.	课本	名词	kèběn	textbook
5.	都	副词	dōu	all, both
6.	同学	名词	tóngxué	classmate

四 主要语言点 Main language points

1 这些是什么?

“些”是表示不定数量的量词，常用在“一”“这”“那”“哪”等词后面。例如：

“些” is a measure word that indicates an indefinite quantity. It is often used after “一”, “这”, “那”, “哪” and so on. For example:

一些　　这些　　那些　　哪些

“这些” 是指示代词，指代两个或两个以上的人或事物，所指代的对象距离说话人比较近。例如：

“这些” is a demonstrative pronoun that refers to two or more persons or things near the speaker. For example:

（1）这些是书。

（2）这些是课本。

视频：12.1 这些是什么？

2 那些也是课本吗？

“那些”也是指示代词，指代两个或两个以上的人或事物，所指代的对象距离说话人比较远。例如：

“那些” is also a demonstrative pronoun, which refers to two or more persons or things far away from the speaker. For example:

（1）那些是我的课本。

（2）那些是同学们的书。

视频：12.1 这些是什么？

3 那些都是同学们的学生证。

“都”表示所说的人或事物全部包括在内，没有一个例外。比如：

“都” indicates that all the persons or things mentioned are included, without exception. For example:

（1）我们都是学生。

（2）那些都是手机。

（3）这些都是课本。

视频：12.1 这些是什么？

五 文化小常识 General knowledge of culture

中国人的重要证件

证件是指用来证明一个人的身份、经历等的证书和文件。例如，学生证证明一个人的学生身份，是证明某人还在学校学习的一种证件。学生出入校园或参加各种活动等大都需要学生证。其他比较重要的证件还有居民身份证、护照、工作证和毕业证等。

Important Certificates of Chinese People

Certificates refer to the credentials or documents used to prove a person's identity, experience, etc. For example, a student ID is used to prove a person's student status, that is, a proof of the fact that someone is still studying in school. Many schools require a student ID for entering and exiting the campus or participating in various activities. Other important certificates include the resident ID card, passport, work certificate, graduation certificate, etc.

六 练习与实践 Exercises and practice

1 听录音，选择你听到的声母，然后跟读三遍。12-3
Listen to the recording and choose the initial you hear, then read the Pinyin three times after the recording.

（1）{z / c / zh} è　　（2）{k / g / h} è　　（3）{t / t / l} óng

2 听录音，选择你听到的韵母和声调，然后跟读三遍。12-4
Listen to the recording and choose the final and tone you hear, then read the Pinyin three times after the recording.

（1）x {ié / iá / ué}　　（2）d {ō / ōu / uó}　　（3）b {ěn / ěng / ǎn}

3 听录音，选择你听到的音，然后朗读下面的拼音。12-5
Listen to the recording and choose the pronunciation you hear, then read the following Pinyin aloud.

（1）谢 xiè — 些 xiē　　（2）哪 nǎ — 那 nà　　（3）这 zhè — 舍 shè

（4）本 běn — 很 hěn　　（5）课 kè — 个 gè　　（6）证 zhèng — 真 zhēn

（7）那些 nàxiē — 哪些 nǎxiē　　（8）个人 gèrén — 课本 kèběn

4 朗读下面的句子，注意语调和重音。

Read the following sentences aloud, paying attention to the intonation and stress.

（1）这些是什么？

（2）这些是课本。

（3）那些也是课本吗？

（4）不是，那些都是学生证。

（5）是谁的学生证呢？

（6）都是同学们的学生证。

5 排列词语成句子。

Arrange the words into sentences.

（1）谁　书　是　那　的

______________________________？

（2）谁　都　课本　的　是　这些

______________________________？

（3）这些　是　的　妈妈　都　书

______________________________。

（4）同学们　那些　是　的　都　课本

______________________________。

6 替换练习：先替换画线的部分，然后和同学一起模仿对话。

Substitution drills: Replace the underlined parts first, then imitate the following dialogues with your classmates.

（1）A：<u>这</u>是什么？

B：<u>这</u>是课本。

那
这些
那些

（2）A：这是谁的课本呢？

B：都是同学们的课本。

那	老师们
这些	他们
那些	朋友们

7 看图完成下面的对话，然后和同学一起演示一下儿对话的内容。
Look at the picture and complete the following dialogue, then act it out with your classmates.

男：________是什么？

女：________是课本。

男：________也是课本吗？

女：________，________是学生证。

8 看视频，先回答问题，然后和同学一起表演视频的内容。
Watch the video and answer the questions. Then act out the video with your classmates.

（1）那些是什么？

（2）那些东西（dōngxi）都是谁的呢？

视频：12.1 这些是什么？

9 汉字练习：看汉字笔画笔顺动态图，并跟着书写。

Practice Chinese characters: Look at the animated illustrations of the strokes and the order of strokes of the following characters, and then write them down.

xiē 些

xué 学

shēng 生

zhèng 证

kè 课

běn 本

dōu 都

tóng 同

第十二课　汉字笔画笔顺动态图

交际项目四

询问时间

第十三课
Lesson 13

Xiànzài jǐ diǎn
现在几点

重点提示

- **交际功能：**谈论时间。
- **主要生词：**现在、几、点、半、分。
- **主要语言点：**用“几点”询问时间，名词谓语句，时间表达方式。
- **文化小常识：**汉语的时间表达方式。

一 看图讨论 Look at the picture and discuss

1. 如果你想知道现在的时间，该怎么问呢？
If you want to know the current time, what should you ask?
2. 如果我们要告诉别人现在的时间，该怎么说呢？
What should we say if we want to tell others the current time?

二 课 文 Text

听录音回答问题 Listen to the recording and answer the following questions.

1. 马文问了什么？ What did Ma Wen ask?
2. 李安平是怎么回答他的？ How did Li Anping answer him?

Xiànzài jǐ diǎn
现在几点 13-1

Mǎ Wén: Xiànzài jǐ diǎn?
马 文：现在 几 点？

Lǐ Ānpíng: Xiànzài bā diǎn.
李 安平：现在 八点。

Mǎ Wén: Wǒmen jǐ diǎn shàngkè?
马 文：我们 几 点 上课？

Lǐ Ānpíng: Wǒmen bā diǎn bàn shàngkè.
李 安平：我们 八 点 半 上课。

Mǎ Wén: Jǐ diǎn xiàkè ne?
马 文：几 点 下课 呢？

Lǐ Ānpíng: Shí diǎn shí fēn xiàkè.
李 安平：十 点 十 分 下课。

三 生词 New words 13-2

1. 现在	名词	xiànzài	now
2. 几	代词	jǐ	what, how many
3. 点	量词	diǎn	o'clock
4. 八	数词	bā	eight
5. 上课	动词	shàngkè	start class
6. 半	数词	bàn	half
7. 下课	动词	xiàkè	finish class
8. 十	数词	shí	ten
9. 分	量词	fēn	minute

四 主要语言点 Main language points

1 现在几点?

"几"一般用来询问十以下的数量。"几点"用来询问时间，注意汉语的语序是"几"在前，"点"在后。例如：

"几" is usually used when inquiring about a number less than 10. "几点" is used to ask about a particular point in time. Note that in Chinese, "几" is used before "点". For example:

（1）几点上课？

（2）你几点下课？

（3）你几点去学校？

视频：13.1 现在几点？

2 现在八点。

这是一个名词谓语句。名词谓语句是由普通名词、名词短语、数量短语、时间名词等做谓语的句子。其语序是"主语 S + 谓语 P"，意思是"S 是 P"，但"是"不出现。名词谓语句除了用于表达时间外，还可以用来表达日期、数量、年龄等。例如：

This is a sentence with a nominal predicate. A sentence in which a common noun, noun phrase, quantitative phrase, or word denoting time is used as the predicate is a sentence with a nominal predicate. Its word order is "Subject (S) + Predicate (P)", meaning "S is P". However, "是" doesn't appear. In addition to indicating time, such a sentence is also used to indicate date, amount, age, etc. For example:

（1）现在十点。

（2）今天星期三（xīngqī sān）。

（3）他十岁（suì）。

视频：13.1 现在几点？

3 十点十分下课。

"× 点 × 分"是汉语表达时间的常用方式。汉语表达时间的词语有"点、分、秒"等。汉语表达时间的语序是从大的时间单位到小的时间单位依次排列，即“点→分→秒”。例如：

“×点×分” is a common expression of a particular point in time in Chinese. Chinese words used to indicate a particular time are “点” “分” “秒”, etc. The word order in the expression of time is from the largest unit to the smallest, namely “点→分→秒”. For example:

（1）现在八点二十五（èrshí wǔ）分三十秒（miǎo）。

（2）他八点三十（sānshí）分上课。

（3）我们十点二十分下课。

如果没有后面的秒数，并且“分”前面的数量大于 10 时，“分”可以不用读出或写出。例如：

If there is no number denoting seconds and the number denoting minutes is larger than 10, the word “分” can be left out when reading or writing the time. For example:

6：25　　读作 / 写作　　六点二十五（liù diǎn èrshíwǔ）

如果“分”前面的数量正好是 30 时，“30 分”可以读作或写作“半”。例如：
If the number denoting minutes is exactly 30, it can be read or written as “半”. For example:

6：30　　读作 / 写作　　六点半（liù diǎn bàn）

如果“分”前面的数量正好是 15 的倍数，几倍就可以读作或写作“几刻”。例如：

If the number denoting minutes is exactly a multiple of 15, it can be read or written as “number + 刻 (quarter)”. For example:

6：15　　读作 / 写作　　六点一刻（liù diǎn yí kè）

如果“分”前面的数量小于30，可以读作或写作“××点过××分”。例如：

If the number denoting minutes is less than 30, it can be read or written as “……点过＋……分”. For example:

6：05　　读作 / 写作　　六点过五分（liù diǎn guò wǔ fēn）

视频：13.2 十点十分下课。

五 文化小常识 General knowledge of culture

汉语的时间表达方式

汉语的时间单位是“点、分、秒”，按照从大到小的顺序（点→分→秒）来读或写。如，6：15：20 读作“六点十五分二十秒”。“点”也可以说成“时”。如，6：15：20 可以说成“六时十五分二十秒”。

The Expression of a Particular Time in Chinese

The Chinese words used to indicate a particular time are: “点, 分, 秒”, etc. A particular time is read or written from the largest unit to the smallest, that is, “点→分→秒”. For example, 6:15:20 is read/written as “liù diǎn shíwǔ fēn èrshí miǎo”. “点” can also be replaced with “时”. For example, 6:15:20 can be read or written as “liù shí shíwǔ fēn èrshí miǎo”.

六 练习与实践 Exercises and practice

1 用汉语读出下面的基数词。
Read the following cardinal numbers in Chinese.

基数词是描述人或事物数量多少的数词，也可以用来比较大小。注意下表中基数词的读法和写法。

A cardinal number is a numeral that describes the number of persons or things. It can also be used to compare the sizes. Note how cardinal numbers are read and written in the table below.

数字	汉字	拼音	数字	汉字	拼音
1	一	yī	11	十一	shíyī
2	二	èr	12	十二	shí'èr
3	三	sān	13	十三	shísān
4	四	sì	14	十四	shísì
5	五	wǔ	15	十五	shíwǔ
6	六	liù	16	十六	shíliù
7	七	qī	17	十七	shíqī
8	八	bā	18	十八	shíbā
9	九	jiǔ	19	十九	shíjiǔ
10	十	shí	20	二十	èrshí

2 听录音，选择你听到的声母，然后跟读三遍。 13-3
Listen to the recording and choose the initial you hear, then read the Pinyin three times after the recording.

（1）{j, q, x} iàn　　（2）{z, c, zh} ài　　（3）{s, x, sh} àng

3 听录音，选择你听到的韵母和声调，然后跟读三遍。 13-4
Listen to the recording and choose the final and tone you hear, then read the Pinyin three times after the recording.

（1）x {à, ià, iào}　　（2）b {àn, àng, èn}　　（3）f {ēn, ēng, ān}

4 听录音，选择你听到的声调，然后跟读三遍。 13-5
Listen to the recording and choose the tone you hear, then read the Pinyin three times after the recording.

（1）ˉ ˊ ˇ ˋ ji　　（2）ˉ ˊ ˇ ˋ dian　　（3）ˉ ˊ ˇ ˋ ba

5 听录音，选择你听到的音，然后朗读下面的拼音。 13-6
Listen to the recording and choose the pronunciation you hear, then read the following Pinyin aloud.

（1）见 jiàn — 现 xiàn　　（2）几 jǐ — 取 qǔ　　（3）刻 kè — 个 gè

（4）上 shàng — 唱 chàng　　（5）钱 qián — 点 diǎn　　（6）谢 xiè — 下 xià

shí chí
（7）十 — 迟

fēng fēn
（8）风 — 分

bàn bān
（9）半 — 班

shàngcài xiànzài
（10）上菜 — 现在

shàngkè chànggē
（11）上课 — 唱歌

6 朗读下面的句子，注意语调和重音。

Read the following sentences aloud, paying attention to the intonation and stress.

（1）现在几点？

（2）现在八点。

（3）你们几点上课？

（4）我们八点半上课。

7 看图填空。

Look at the pictures and fill in the following blanks.

（1）现在__________。　　（2）我们__________下课。

8 排列词语成句子。

Arrange the words into sentences.

（1）几　点　现在

________________________________？

（2）八　点　现在　半

________________________________。

（3）上课　几　你们　点

________________________________？

（4）我们　上课　二十　八　点

________________________________。

9 看视频，先回答问题，然后和同学一起表演视频的内容。

Watch the video and answer the questions. Then act out the video with your classmates.

（1）他们几点上课？
（2）他们几点下课？

视频：13.2 十点十分下课。

10 给同学们介绍一下儿你自己的日常活动时间，注意用上下面的词语。

Tell your classmates about your own daily schedule of activities. Use the following words.

……点……分　半　上课　下课

11 汉字练习：看汉字笔画笔顺动态图，并跟着书写。

Practice Chinese characters: Look at the animated illustrations of the strokes and the order of strokes of the following characters, and then write them down.

xiàn
现

zài	jǐ	diǎn	bā	bàn	xià	shí	fēn
在	几	点	八	半	下	十	分

第十三课　汉字笔画笔顺动态图

第十四课

Lesson 14

Jīntiān xīngqī jǐ

今天星期几

重点提示

- **交际功能：** 谈论一个星期中某一天的日期。
- **主要生词：** 今天、星期、明天、下、个。
- **主要语言点：** 用“几”询问一个星期中某一天的日期，一周时间的表达方法，表示次序的“下个”。
- **文化小常识：** 中国人的周末生活。

一 看图讨论 Look at the picture and discuss

1. 你想知道今天星期几，用汉语怎么问呢？

   You want to know what day it is today. How can you ask it in Chinese?

2. 你想告诉别人今天星期几，用汉语怎么回答呢？

   You want to tell others what day it is today. How will you answer it in Chinese?

二 课 文 Text

听录音回答问题 Listen to the recording and answer the following questions.

1. 马文问了什么？ What did Ma Wen ask?
2. 李安平是怎么回答的？ How did Li Anping answer him?

Jīntiān xīngqī jǐ
今天星期几 14-1

Mǎ Wén: Jīntiān xīngqī jǐ?
马　文：今天星期几？

Lǐ Ānpíng: Jīntiān xīngqīliù.
李安平：今天 星期六。

Mǎ Wén: Míngtiān xīngqī jǐ?
马　文：明天 星期几？

Lǐ Ānpíng: Míngtiān xīngqītiān.
李安平：明天 星期天。

Mǎ Wén: Wǒmen xīngqī jǐ kǎoshì?
马　文：我们 星期几考试？

Lǐ Ānpíng: Wǒmen xià gè xīngqīyī kǎoshì.
李安平：我们 下 个 星期一考试。

三 生词 New words 14-2

1.	今天	名词	jīntiān	today
2.	星期	名词	xīngqī	week
3.	星期六	名词	xīngqīliù	Saturday
4.	明天	名词	míngtiān	tomorrow
5.	星期天	名词	xīngqītiān	Sunday
6.	考试	动词	kǎoshì	have an examination
7.	下	名词	xià	next
8.	个	量词	gè	*a measure word used before nouns without a particular measure word of their own*
9.	星期一	名词	xīngqīyī	Monday

四 主要语言点 Main language points

1 今天星期几？

“几”可以用来询问一个星期中某一天的日期，这种问句中的“几”只能跟在“星期”的后面。例如：

“几” can be used to ask which day it is of a week. “几” in such interrogative sentences can only be used after “星期”. For example:

（1）后天（hòutiān）星期几？
（2）我们星期几考试？
（3）你们星期几去北京（Běijīng）？

视频：14.1 今天星期几？

2 今天星期六。

汉语中，除了星期天外，一个星期中的其余六天依次是在“星期”后分别加上数字“一”至“六”构成。注意汉语的词序是“星期”在前，数字在后。例如：

In Chinese, except Sunday, the other six days of a week are expressed using the following pattern: “星期 + one of the numbers from 一 to 六”. Note the word order in Chinese: “星期” is used before the number. For example:

（1）今天星期二。

（2）明天星期三。

（3）后天星期四。

星期一	星期二	星期三	星期四	星期五	星期六	星期日
Monday	Tuesday	Wednesday	Thursday	Friday	Saturday	Sunday

视频：14.1 今天星期几？

3 我们下个星期一考试。

“下个”指接着某个人或某事物的另一个。例如：

“下个” indicates another one that is next to someone or something. For example:

（1）我们下个星期去中国。

（2）端午节（Duānwǔ Jié）是下个星期一。

视频：14.2 我们星期几考试？

五 文化小常识 General knowledge of culture

中国人的周末生活

中国人的周末活动丰富多样。很多人周末到郊区去旅游休假，亲近自然。也有不少人利用周末进行体育锻炼或参加文化艺术活动，如看电影、听音乐会、参观展览馆和博物馆等。不过，也有不少人周末的时候还在工作，如各大商场、酒店等都照常营业。

Chinese People's Weekend Life

Chinese people's weekend activities are rich in variety. Many people spend their weekends in the suburbs to be close to nature. Many others use weekends to take exercise, participate in cultural or artistic activities, such as seeing films, going to concerts, visiting exhibition centers and museums and so on. However, there are still many people working on weekends, such as those working in shopping malls and hotels.

六 练习与实践 Exercises and practice

1 用汉语读出下面的序数词。
Read the following ordinal numbers in Chinese.

序数词是指表示顺序的数词。汉语序数词的读/写方法是在相应的基数词前面加“第”。注意下表中序数词的读法和写法。

Ordinal numbers refer to numerals indicating order. The way to read or write a Chinese ordinal number is to use “第” before the corresponding cardinal number. Note how the ordinal numbers in the table below are read and written.

基数	序数	拼音	基数	序数	拼音
1	第一	dì-yī	12	第十二	dì-shí’èr
2	第二	dì-èr	13	第十三	dì-shísān
3	第三	dì-sān	14	第十四	dì-shísì
4	第四	dì-sì	15	第十五	dì-shíwǔ
5	第五	dì-wǔ	16	第十六	dì-shíliù
6	第六	dì-liù	17	第十七	dì-shíqī
7	第七	dì-qī	18	第十八	dì-shíbā
8	第八	dì-bā	19	第十九	dì-shíjiǔ
9	第九	dì-jiǔ	20	第二十	dì-èrshí
10	第十	dì-shí	30	第三十	dì-sānshí
11	第十一	dì-shíyī	100	第一百	dì-yìbǎi

2 听录音，选择你听到的声母，然后跟读三遍。 14-3
Listen to the recording and choose the initial you hear, then read the Pinyin three times after the recording.

（1）d / t / l } iān　　（2）j / q / x } ī　　（3）x / s / sh } ì

3 听录音，选择你听到的韵母和声调，然后跟读三遍。 14-4
Listen to the recording and choose the final and tone you hear, then read the Pinyin three times after the recording.

（1）l { uì / iù / ù　　（2）x { īn / īng / iā　　（3）x { ià / iào / ào

4 听录音，选择你听到的声调，然后跟读三遍。 14-5
Listen to the recording and choose the tone you hear, then read the Pinyin three times after the recording.

（1）ˉ ˊ ˇ ˋ kao　　（2）ˉ ˊ ˇ ˋ ming　　（3）ˉ ˊ ˇ ˋ ge

5 听录音，选择你听到的音，然后朗读下面的拼音。 14-6
Listen to the recording and choose the pronunciation you hear, then read the following Pinyin aloud.

（1）今 jīn — 心 xīn　　（2）千 qiān — 天 tiān　　（3）星 xīng — 新 xīn

（4）期 qī — 西 xī　　（5）明 míng — 民 mín　　（6）好 hǎo — 考 kǎo

jīntiān xìng Tián
（7）今天 — 姓 田

xīn jī xīngqī
（8）新机 — 星期

hǎo shì kǎoshì
（9）好 事 — 考试

xià gè xiàkè
（10）下 个 — 下课

6 朗读下面的句子，注意语调和重音。

Read the following sentences aloud, paying attention to the intonation and stress.

（1）今天星期几？
（2）今天星期六。
（3）明天星期几？
（4）明天星期天。
（5）我们星期几考试？

7 替换练习。

Substitution drills

（1）<u>今天</u>星期几？

明天
昨天（zuótiān）
后天

（2）今天星期<u>一</u>。

二
六
天

（3）我们下个星期<u>三</u>考试。

五
二
四

8 排列词语成句子。

Arrange the words into sentences.

(1) 几　今天　星期

________________?

(2) 考试　几　我们　星期

________________?

(3) 下　个　我们　考试　星期一

________________。

(4) 他　有　星期一　课

________________。

9 看表完成下面的对话，并和同学一起模仿对话。

Look at the table to complete the dialogue below, and imitate the dialogue with your classmates.

星期一	星期二	星期三	星期四	星期五	星期六	星期天
			1 今天	2	3 上课	4
5 考试	6	7	8	9	10	11
12	13	14	15	16	17	18
19	20	21	22	23	24	25
26	27	28	29	30	31	

（今天星期四）

A：你________________上课吗？

B：我________________上课。

A：你什么时候考试？

B：我________________考试。

10 看视频，先回答问题，然后和同学一起表演视频的内容。

Watch the video and answer the questions. Then act out the video with your classmates.

（1）男生问了什么？
（2）女生回答了什么？

视频：14.2 我们星期几考试？

11 和同学说说自己近两个星期的活动计划，注意用上下面的词语。

Talk to your classmates about your activity plan for the next two weeks. Use the following words.

今天　　星期　　考试　　下个　　上课

12 汉字练习：看汉字笔画笔顺动态图，并跟着书写。

Practice Chinese characters: Look at the animated illustrations of the strokes and the order of strokes of the following characters, and then write them down.

jīn
今

tiān
天

xīng
星

qī
期

liù
六

míng
明

kǎo
考

shì
试

gè
个

第十四课 汉字笔画笔顺动态图

第十五课
Lesson 15

Nǐ de shēngrì shì jǐ yuè jǐ hào
你的生日是几月几号

重点提示

- **交际功能：** 谈论日期。
- **主要生词：** 生日、月、号、农历、公历。
- **主要语言点：** 用“几”询问日期，汉语的日期表达方法，反问句“不是……吗”。
- **文化小常识：** 公历和农历。

一 看图讨论 Look at the picture and discuss

1. 他们在做什么？ What are they doing?
2. 他们可能说什么呢？ What might they say?

二 课文 Text

听录音回答问题 Listen to the recording and answer the following questions.

1. 马文问了什么？ What did Ma Wen ask?
2. 李安平是怎么回答他的？ How did Li Anping answer him?

Nǐ de shēngrì shì jǐ yuè jǐ hào
你的生日是几月几号 15-1

Mǎ Wén: Nǐ de shēngrì shì jǐ yuè jǐ hào?
马 文：你的生日是几月几号？

Lǐ Ānpíng: Wǒ de shēngrì shì wǔ yuè wǔ hào.
李安平：我的生日是五月五号。

Mǎ Wén: Shì Duānwǔ Jié nà tiān ma?
马 文：是端午节那天吗？

Lǐ Ānpíng: Bú shì Duānwǔ Jié.
李安平：不是端午节。

Mǎ Wén: Duānwǔ Jié bú shì wǔ yuè wǔ hào ma?
马 文：端午节不是五月五号吗？

Lǐ Ānpíng: Bú shì, Duānwǔ Jié shì nónglì wǔ yuè chū wǔ. Wǒ de shēngrì shì gōnglì wǔ yuè wǔ hào.
李安平：不是，端午节是农历五月初五。我的生日是公历五月五号。

三 生 词 New words 15-2

1.	生日	名词	shēngrì	birthday
2.	月	名词	yuè	month
3.	号	名词	hào	*referring to a date of a month*
4.	五号		wǔ hào	the fifth day of a month
5.	端午节	专有名词	Duānwǔ Jié	Dragon Boat Festival
	节	名词	jié	festival
6.	初五		chū wǔ	the fifth day of a lunar month
7.	农历	名词	nónglì	lunar calendar
8.	公历	名词	gōnglì	Gregorian calendar

四 主要语言点 Main language points

1 你的生日是几月几号?

"几"可以用来询问日期，即用来询问某年或某月中的某一天。注意，这种问句中的"几"要放在"月""号 / 日"的前面。例如：

"几" can be used to ask about the date in a year or month. Note that "几" in such interrogative sentences should be placed before "月" and "号/日". For example:

(1) 今天几月几号?
(2) 明天几月几号?
(3) 我们几月几号考试?

视频：15.1 你的生日是几月几号?

2 我的生日是五月五号。

"× 月 × 号"是汉语日期的常见表达方式。汉语表达日期的词语从大的时间单位到小的时间单位依次是:"年→月→号 / 日"。例如:

"× 月× 号" is a common expression of a date in Chinese. The Chinese words indicating a date are used from the largest unit to the smallest, that is, "年→月→号/日". For example:

(1)今天是十月一号 / 日。

(2)妈妈的生日是六月二十号 / 日。

"日"和"号"都表示某一天,"日"多用于书面语,"号"多用于口语。

Both "日" and "号" indicate a day in Chinese. "日" is mostly used in written Chinese, and "号" is mostly used in spoken Chinese.

视频:15.1 你的生日是几月几号?

3 端午节不是五月五号吗?

"……不是……吗"是一个反问句。这种问句有强调肯定的作用,不要求回答。例如:

"……不是……吗" is a rhetorical question. Such interrogative sentences are used to emphasize affirmation, and no reply is required. For example:

(1)明天不是星期天吗?

(2)这不是他的书吗?

(3)那不是马文吗?

视频:15.2 端午节不是五月五号吗?

五 文化小常识 General knowledge of culture

公历和农历

在中国，人们同时使用两种日历：一种是世界通用的公历，另一种是中国传统的农历。农历综合考虑了太阳、地球和月亮三者之间的关系来记时。中国传统的农历将一年分为24个节气，帮助人们安排农业生产活动。汉语中，这两种日历使用的单位都是“年、月、号（日）”，按照时间单位从大到小的顺序依次读作或写作“× 年→ × 月→ × 号（日）”。

Gregorian Calendar and Lunar Calendar

In China, two kinds of calendars are used. One is the Gregorian calendar used all over the world, and the other is the traditional Chinese lunar calendar. The lunar calendar comprehensively considers the relationship among the sun, the earth and the moon to record time. The traditional Chinese lunar calendar divides a year into 24 solar terms to help people arrange agricultural production activities. In Chinese, the units used in both types of calendars are “年”, “月”, “号 (日)”, and they are read and written in descending order: “× 年 → × 月 → × 号 (日)”.

六 练习与实践 Exercises and practice

1 听录音，选择你听到的声母，然后跟读三遍。15-3
Listen to the recording and choose the initial you hear, then read the Pinyin three times after the recording.

（1）s / sh / x + ēng　（2）k / g / h + ào　（3）c / q / ch + ū

2 听录音，选择你听到的韵母和声调，然后跟读三遍。15-4
Listen to the recording and choose the final and tone you hear, then read the Pinyin three times after the recording.

（1）y + èi / iè / uè　（2）g + āng / ēng / ōng　（3）d + uēn / ān / uān

3 听录音，选择你听到的声调，然后跟读三遍。15-5
Listen to the recording and choose the tone you hear, then read the Pinyin three times after the recording.

（1）ˉ ˊ ˇ ˋ nong　（2）ˉ ˊ ˇ ˋ wu　（3）ˉ ˊ ˇ ˋ jie

4 听录音，选择你听到的音，然后朗读下面的拼音。15-6
Listen to the recording and choose the pronunciation you hear, then read the following Pinyin aloud.

（1）duān 端 — huān 欢　（2）jìn 进 — qìng 庆　（3）hǎo 好 — hào 号

（4）wǔ 午 — wǒ 我　（5）jié 节 — jiě 姐　（6）xiē 些 — yuè 月

shēngzì shēngrì
（7）生字 — 生日

Duānwǔ shàngwǔ
（8）端午 — 上午

gōnglì gōnglǐ
（9）公历 — 公里

nǔlì nónglì
（10）努力 — 农历

5 朗读下面的句子，注意语调和重音。

Read the following sentences aloud, paying attention to the intonation and stress.

（1）你的生日是几月几号？
（2）我的生日是五月五号。
（3）是端午节那天吗？
（4）不是端午节。
（5）端午节不是五月五号吗？

6 看图填空，然后用汉语说出具体的日期。

Look at the pictures and fill in the blanks, and then tell the dates in Chinese.

（1）____月____日　（2）____月____日　（3）____月____日

（4）____月____日　（5）____月____日　（6）____月____日

7 替换练习。
Substitution drills

(1) 我的生日是三月十一号。

他	八月二十三号
妈妈	十月二十号
马文	十一月十八号

(2) 端午节是农历五月初五。

今天	八月十五
星期一	九月初一
星期天	十一月二十五

8 排列词语成句子。
Arrange the words into sentences.

(1) 你 几 的 是 几 月 生日 号

_______________________________________?

(2) 今天 吗 不 五 月 是 号 五

_______________________________________?

(3) 星期 吗 不 考试 是 有 下个 五

_______________________________________?

(4) 生日 的 一月 妈妈 是 十七 日

_______________________________________。

9 看视频，先回答问题，然后和同学一起表演视频的内容。
Watch the video and answer the questions. Then act out the video with your classmates.

(1) 男生问了什么？

（2）女生回答了什么？

视频：15.1 你的生日是几月几号？

10 说说你自己和家庭成员的生日是哪天，注意用上下面的词语。

Talk about the dates of your own birthday and your family members' birthdays. Use the following words.

生日　　月　　日　　号　　公历　　农历　　初

11 汉字练习：看汉字笔画笔顺动态图，并跟着书写。

Practice Chinese characters: Look at the animated illustrations of the strokes and the order of strokes of the following characters, and then write them down.

rì 日

yuè 月

hào 号

wǔ 五

duān 端

wǔ
午

jié
节

chū
初

nóng
农

lì
历

gōng
公

第十五课 汉字笔画笔顺动态图

交际项目五

寻找位置

第十六课

Lesson 16

Túshūguǎn zài nǎr

图书馆在哪儿

重点提示

- **交际功能：** 寻找和介绍简单的位置。
- **主要生词：** 在、哪儿、前面、右边。
- **主要语言点：** 表示处所的“在”，疑问代词“哪儿”，方位名词“前、后、左、右”等。
- **文化小常识：** 汉语简单方位的表达方式。

一 看图讨论 Look at the picture and discuss

1. 他们在做什么？ What are they doing?
2. 他们会说什么呢？ What might they say?

二 课文 Text

听录音回答问题 Listen to the recording and answer the following questions.

1. 男生在找什么地方？他是怎么问的？

   What place was the boy student looking for? How did he ask?

2. 女生是怎么回答他的？ How did the girl student answer him?

Túshūguǎn zài nǎr

图书馆在哪儿 16–1

Mǎ Wén: Nín hǎo! Qǐngwèn, túshūguǎn zài nǎr?

马 文：您好！请问，图书馆在哪儿？

lùrén: Qiánmiàn shì túshūguǎn.

路人：前面是图书馆。

Mǎ Wén: Yòubian shì shénme?

马 文：右边是什么？

lùrén: Yòubian shì jiàoxuélóu.

路人：右边是教学楼。

Mǎ Wén: Xièxie!

马 文：谢谢！

lùrén: Bú kèqi!

路人：不客气！

三 生 词 New words 16-2

1.	图书馆	名词	túshūguǎn	library
2.	在	动词	zài	be located (in, on, at...)
3.	哪儿	代词	nǎr	where
4.	路人	名词	lùrén	passer-by
5.	前面	名词	qiánmiàn	front
6.	右边	名词	yòubian	right (side)
7.	教学楼	名词	jiàoxuélóu	teaching building

四 主要语言点 Main language points

1 请问，图书馆在哪儿?

句子中的"在"表示某人或某事物的方位或处所。常用的肯定表达形式是：

名词（表示人或事物）/ 代词 + 在 + 方位词 / 处所词语

"在" in this sentence indicates the location or position of somebody or something. The common affirmative form is:

Noun (Somebody/Something)/Pronoun + 在 + Noun of Direction or Locality

例如：

For example:

（1）教学楼在前面。
（2）图书馆在左边。
（3）他在图书馆。

句子中的“哪儿”是疑问代词，用来询问地方，用在句子的开头、中间、结尾都可以。常用的疑问表达形式是：

名词（表示人或事物）/ 代词 + 在 + 哪儿？

“哪儿” in this sentence is an interrogative pronoun used to ask about locality, and it can be used either at the beginning, in the middle, or end of a sentence. The common interrogative form is:

Noun (Somebody/Something)/Pronoun + 在 + 哪儿？

例如：
For example:

（1）教学楼在哪儿？
（2）他们在哪儿？
（3）学生证在哪儿？
（4）哪儿有课本？
（5）他在哪儿上课？

视频：16.1 图书馆在哪儿？

2 前面是图书馆。

“前面”是一个表示方位的名词。汉语常用的方位词有“前、后、左、右、上、下、里、外、前面、后面、左边、右边、上面、下面、里面、外面”等。

例如：

"前面" is a noun of direction or locality. Commonly used nouns of direction or locality in Chinese include "前", "后", "左", "右", "上", "下", "里", "外", "前面", "后面", "左边", "右边", "上面", "下面", "里面", "外面" and so on. For example:

（1）我的前面是马文。

（2）老师在我的右边。

（3）图书馆在前面。

视频：16.1 图书馆在哪儿？

五 文化小常识 General knowledge of culture

汉语简单方位的表达方式

汉语的方位词"前、后、左、右"一般表示相对简单的方位。也就是说，当我们用"前、后、左、右"来说出某人或某事物的位置或者方向时，这种方位一般相对比较近，并且涉及的范围比较小。这些方位词还可以组合起来，用在特定的时间、数量之后，表示大概的范围，如"八点前后""三十岁左右"等。

Simple Expressions of Direction or Locality in Chinese

The Chinese nouns of direction or locality "前", "后", "左", and "右" are usually used to indicate simple direction or locality. In other words, when we say "前", "后", "左", "右" to describe the position or location of somebody or something, it is usually near and involves a small scope. These nouns of direction or locality can also be combined and used after some specific time and quantity to indicate a rough scope, such as "八点前后", "三十岁左右" and so on.

六 练习与实践 Exercises and practice

1 听录音，选择你听到的音，然后朗读下面的拼音。16-3

Listen to the recording and choose the pronunciation you hear, then read the following Pinyin aloud.

（1）图 tú — 读 dú	（2）菜 cài — 在 zài	（3）前 qián — 点 diǎn
（4）楼 lóu — 走 zǒu	（5）转 zhuǎn — 馆 guǎn	（6）边 biān — 面 miàn
（7）教学 jiàoxué — 小学 xiǎoxué	（8）那儿 nàr — 哪儿 nǎr	

2 朗读下面的句子，注意语调和重音。

Read the following sentences aloud, paying attention to the intonation and stress.

（1）请问，图书馆在哪儿？
（2）前面是图书馆。
（3）右边是什么？
（4）右边是教学楼。

3 替换练习：先替换画线的部分，然后和同学一起模仿对话。

Substitution drills: Replace the underlined parts first, then imitate the following dialogues with your classmates.

（1）A：请问<u>图书馆</u>在哪儿？

　　B：图书馆在<u>前面</u>。

教学楼　　　　　　　　　　后面（hòumiàn）
办公楼（bàngōnglóu）　　　右边
宿舍楼（sùshèlóu）　　　　左边（zuǒbian）

（2）A：请问<u>右边</u>是什么？

　　B：<u>右边</u>是宿舍楼。

左边
后面
前面

4 以你自己为中心，用下面的词语介绍一下儿你身边同学的位置。

Take yourself as the center, and use the following words to introduce the positions of the classmates around you.

在　　前面　　后面　　左边　　右边

5 看视频，先回答问题，然后和同学一起表演视频的内容。

Watch the video and answer the questions. Then act out the video with your classmates.

（1）图书馆在哪儿？

（2）教学楼在哪儿？

视频：16.1 图书馆在哪儿？

6 汉字练习：看汉字笔画笔顺动态图，并跟着书写。

Practice Chinese characters: Look at the animated illustrations of the strokes and the order of strokes of the following characters, and then write them down.

tú
图

guǎn
馆

qián
前

miàn
面

yòu
右

bian
边

jiào
教

lóu
楼

第十六课　汉字笔画笔顺动态图

第十七课 Lesson 17

Nǎr yǒu dìtiězhàn

哪儿有地铁站

重点提示

- **交际功能：**寻找和介绍比较复杂的位置。
- **主要生词：**地铁站、那边、有、中国银行、旁边。
- **主要语言点：**表示存在的“有”，指示代词“那边”，方位名词“旁边”。
- **文化小常识：**地铁简介。

一 看图讨论 Look at the picture and discuss

1. 他们在做什么？ What are they doing?
2. 他们会说什么呢？ What might they say?

二 课文 Text

听录音回答问题 Listen to the recording and answer the following questions.

1. 男生在找什么地方？他是怎么问的？

   What place was the boy student looking for? How did he ask?

2. 女生是怎么回答他的？ How did the girl student answer him?

Nǎr yǒu dìtiězhàn

哪儿有地铁站 17-1

Mǎ Wén： Nín hǎo! Qǐngwèn, nǎr yǒu dìtiězhàn?
马　文：您好！请问，哪儿有地铁站？

lùrén： Nàbiān yǒu yí gè dìtiězhàn.
路人：那边有一个地铁站。

Mǎ Wén： Zài nǎr ne?
马　文：在哪儿呢？

lùrén： Zài Zhōngguó Yínháng de pángbiān.
路人：在中国银行的旁边。

Mǎ Wén： Xièxie!
马　文：谢谢！

lùrén： Bú kèqi!
路人：不客气！

三 生 词 New words 17-2

1.	地铁站	名词	dìtiězhàn	subway station
	地铁	名词	dìtiě	subway, metro
	站	名词	zhàn	station
2.	那边	代词	nàbiān	over there
3.	有	动词	yǒu	there is
4.	中国银行	专有名词	Zhōngguó Yínháng	Bank of China
	中国	专有名词	Zhōngguó	China
	银行	名词	yínháng	bank
5.	旁边	名词	pángbiān	beside

四 主要语言点 Main language points

1 请问，哪儿有地铁站?

这个句子的“有”是一个表示存在的动词，即表示什么地方存在什么人或什么事物。例如：

“有” in this sentence is a verb used to indicate existence, namely indicating there is somebody or something in some place. For example:

（1）书包（shūbāo）里（li）有书。

（2）图书馆里有很多人。

（3）教学楼前面有一个学生。

视频：17.1 哪儿有地铁站？

2 那边有一个地铁站。

"那边"是一个表示处所的指示代词，指离说话人比较远的位置。例如：

"那边" is a demonstrative pronoun used to indicate a place, referring to a location far away from the speaker. For example:

（1）那边有一个书店（shūdiàn）。

（2）那边有人。

（3）图书馆在那边。

视频：17.1 哪儿有地铁站？

3 在中国银行的旁边。

"旁边"是一个表示方位的名词，指距离某人或某物比较近的位置。例如：

"旁边" is a noun used to indicate direction or locality, referring to a position near someone or something. For example:

（1）老师在我的旁边。

（2）学校旁边有地铁站。

（3）我的旁边是小王。

视频：17.1 哪儿有地铁站？

五 文化小常识 General knowledge of culture

地铁简介

“地铁”是指在地下修建的一种铁路。地铁的优点是：（1）不会堵车，因此很准时；（2）没有污染，很环保；（3）建在地下，节约城市地面空间；（4）运行速度快，客运量大。现在，中国很多城市都有地铁，城市出行非常方便。

Brief Introduction to the Subway

The subway is a kind of railway built underground. The advantages of the subway are: (1) It won't be stuck in traffic jams and is very punctual; (2) It has no pollution and is very eco-friendly; (3) It is built underground to save urban ground space; (4) It has a high running speed and large passenger volume. Now, many cities in China have subways, which makes urban travel very convenient.

六 练习与实践 Exercises and practice

1 听录音，选择你听到的音，然后朗读下面的拼音。 17-3
Listen to the recording and choose the pronunciation you hear, then read the following Pinyin aloud.

（1）铁（tiě）— 写（xiě）　（2）站（zhàn）— 半（bàn）　（3）行（háng）— 旁（páng）

（4）地铁（dìtiě）— 地点（dìdiǎn）　（5）音长（yīncháng）— 银行（yínháng）

（6）那边（nàbiān）— 哪边（nǎ bian）　（7）中国（Zhōngguó）— 总共（zǒnggòng）

2 朗读下面的句子，注意语调和重音。

Read the following sentences aloud, paying attention to the intonation and stress.

（1）您好！请问，哪儿有地铁站？

（2）那边有一个地铁站。

（3）在哪儿呢？

（4）在中国银行的旁边。

3 看图完成下面的对话，然后和同学一起演示对话的内容。

Look at the pictures and complete the following dialogues, then act out the dialogues with your classmates.

（1）A：地铁站________有什么？

　　B：地铁站________ ________很多树（shù）。

（2）A：地铁站在_______？

B：地铁站_______公交（gōngjiāo）站的_______。

4 替换练习：先替换画线的部分，然后和同学一起模仿对话。

Substitution drills: Replace the underlined parts first, then imitate the following dialogues with your classmates.

（1）A：请问，哪儿有地铁站？

B：那边有一个地铁站。

- 书店 / 前面
- 银行 / 后面
- 商店（shāngdiàn） / 左边

（2）A：在哪儿呢？

B：在书店的旁边。

- 学校
- 公园（gōngyuán）
- 公交站

5 给同学介绍一下儿你家或学校周围的单位或建筑物，注意用上下面的词语。

Introduce the places or buildings around your home or school to your classmates. Use the following words.

有　　旁边　　前面　　左边　　右边　　后面

6 看视频，先填空。然后和同学一起表演视频的内容。

Watch the video and fill in the blanks. Then act out the video with your classmates.

A：您好！请问，哪儿______地铁站？

B：那边______一个地铁站。

A：______哪儿呢？

B：______中国银行的______。

视频：17.1哪儿有地铁站？

7 汉字练习：看汉字笔画笔顺动态图，并跟着书写。

Practice Chinese characters: Look at the animated illustrations of the strokes and the order of strokes of the following characters, and then write them down.

dì
地

tiě
铁

zhàn
站

zhōng
中

yín
银

háng
行

páng
旁

第十七课　汉字笔画笔顺动态图

第十八课
Lesson 18

Fùjìn yǒu yínháng ma
附近有银行吗

重点提示

- **交际功能**：寻找和介绍较远的位置。
- **主要生词**：附近、东边、怎么、往、拐。
- **主要语言点**：方位词“东、南、西、北”等，疑问代词“怎么”，介词“往”。
- **文化小常识**：汉语复杂方位的表达方式。

一 看图讨论 Look at the picture and discuss

1. 她们在做什么？ What are they doing?
2. 她们会说什么呢？ What might they say?

二 课 文 Text

听录音回答问题 Listen to the recording and answer the following questions.

1. 男生在找什么地方？他是怎么问的？
   What place was the boy student looking for? How did he ask?
2. 女生是怎么回答他的？ How did the girl student answer him?

Fùjìn yǒu yínháng ma
附近有 银行吗 18-1

Mǎ Wén: Nín hǎo! Qǐngwèn, fùjìn yǒu yínháng ma?
马　文：您好！请问，附近有 银行吗？

lùrén: Yǒu.
路人：有。

Mǎ Wén: Zài nǎr ne?
马　文：在哪儿呢？

lùrén: Zài Xuéxiào de dōngbian.
路人：在学校的东边。

Mǎ Wén: Zěnme zǒu ne?
马　文：怎么走呢？

lùrén: Zài xuéxiào de dōng mén wǎng yòu guǎi sān bǎi mǐ.
路人：在学校的东 门 往 右 拐 三百米。

Mǎ Wén: Xièxie!
马　文：谢谢！

lùrén: Bú kèqi!
路人：不客气！

三 生词 New words 18-2

1.	附近	名词	fùjìn	nearby
2.	学校	名词	xuéxiào	school
3.	东边	名词	dōngbian	east (side)
4.	怎么	代词	zěnme	how
5.	走	动词	zǒu	walk, go
6.	东门		dōng mén	east gate
7.	往	介词	wǎng	toward
8.	拐	动词	guǎi	turn, change direction
9.	百	数词	bǎi	hundred
10.	米	量词	mǐ	meter

四 主要语言点 Main language points

1（银行）在学校的东边。

“东边”是一个表示方位的名词，指太阳升起的那边。汉语中类似的方位名词有“东、南（nán）、西（xī）、北（běi）、东边、南边、西边、北边、东南、西南、东北、西北”等。

“东边” is a noun used to indicate direction or locality, referring to the side where the sun rises. Similar words of locality in Chinese include “东，南，西，

北，东边，南边，西边，北边，东南，西南，东北，西北", etc.

▶ 视频：18.1 附近有银行吗？

2 怎么走呢？

这个句子中的"怎么"是一个疑问代词，用于"怎么 + 动词"的格式中，用来询问做某事的方式。例如：

The word "怎么" in this sentence is an interrogative pronoun used in "怎么 + V" to ask how to do something. For example:

（1）去办公楼怎么走呢？

（2）我们怎么去呢？

（3）去图书馆怎么走呢？

▶ 视频：18.1 附近有银行吗？

3 在学校的东门往右拐三百米。

这里的"往"用于"往 + 方位词 / 地点"的格式中，整个格式在句子中作状语，用来表示动作的方向。例如：

"往" is used in "往 + Noun of Direction or Locality". This structure is used as an adverbial in the sentence to show the direction of an action. For example:

（1）你在前面往左拐。

（2）往前走三百米。

（3）他往中国银行走去。

▶ 视频：18.1 附近有银行吗？

五 文化小常识 General knowledge of culture

汉语复杂方位的表达方式

汉语的方位词“东、西、南、北”等主要用来表示复杂的方位。这种方位一般距离说话人比较远，并且涉及的范围比较大。其中，太阳升起的方位是东边，太阳落山的方位是西边。人面向太阳时，左手的那边是北边，右手的那边是南边。注意，汉语中只能说“东南、西南、东北、西北”，不能说“南东、南西、北东、北西”。

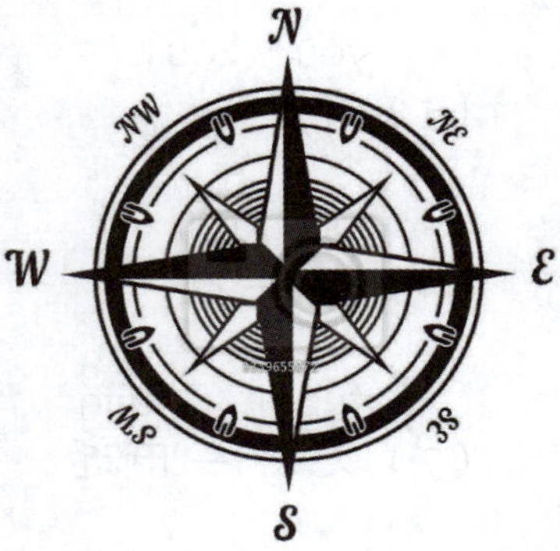

Complex Expressions of Direction or Locality in Chinese

The Chinese nouns of direction or locality “东”, “西”, “南”, and “北” are mainly used to show complex direction or locality, which are usually very far and involve a large scope. Among them, the direction from which the sun rises is east, and the direction towards which the sun sets is west. When a person faces the rising sun, his left-hand side is north, and his right-hand side is south. Note that in Chinese, people only use “东南”, “西南”, “东北”, “西北”, but not “南东”, “南西”, “北东”, or “北西”.

六 练习与实践 Exercises and practice

1 听录音，选择你听到的音，然后朗读下面的拼音。 18-3
Listen to the recording and choose the pronunciation you hear, then read the following Pinyin aloud.

yǒu zǒu （1）有 — 走	jiāo jiā （2）交 — 家	wǎng wáng （3）往 — 王
guǎi gǎi （4）拐 — 改	bù fù （5）不 — 附	dòng dōng （6）动 — 东
fùqīn fùjìn （7）父亲 — 附近	yínháng Yīng-Hàn （8）银行 — 英汉	
zěnme zǒule （9）怎么 — 走了	tóngmén dōng mén （10）同门 — 东 门	

2 朗读下面的句子，注意停顿和重音。
Read the following sentences aloud, paying attention to the pause and stress.

（1）请问，附近有银行吗？
（2）在哪儿呢？
（3）银行在学校的东边。
（4）怎么走呢？
（5）在学校的东门往右拐三百米。

3 看图，先填空，然后早上起来后自己试一试。

Look at the picture and fill in the blanks, then try it yourself after you get up in the morning.

早上起来，面向太阳。

前边是________，后边是________；

左边是________，右边是________。

4 看下面的标志图，先填空，然后用汉语告诉其他同学。

Look at the signs below and fill in the blanks, then tell other classmates the directions in Chinese.

（1）____________ （2）____________ （3）____________

5 替换练习。

Substitution drills

（1）你好，附近有银行吗？	酒店（jiǔdiàn） 书店 地铁站
（2）在南门往右拐。	东 西 北

6 仿照例子，说说你们国家和别的国家的位置关系。

Imitate the example and talk about the positional relationship between your country and other countries.

例如：新加坡（Xīnjiāpō）在中国的南边。

7 说说从教室去图书馆怎么走，注意用上下面的词语。

Tell how to get to the library from your classroom. Use the following words.

东　南　西　北　往　左　右　拐　百　米

8 看视频，先回答问题，然后和同学一起表演视频的内容。

Watch the video and answer the questions. Then act out the video with your classmates.

（1）男生问了什么？

（2）女生回答了什么？

视频：18.1 附近有银行吗？

9 汉字练习：看汉字笔画笔顺动态图，并跟着书写。

Practice Chinese characters: Look at the animated illustrations of the strokes and the order of strokes of the following characters, and then write them down.

fù
附

xiào
校

dōng
东

zěn
怎

mén
门

wǎng
往

guǎi
拐

bǎi
百

mǐ
米

第十八课　汉字笔画笔顺动态图

交际项目六

换钱购物

第十九课 Lesson 19

Wǒ xiǎng huàn yìdiǎnr qián
我想换一点儿钱

重点提示

- **交际功能：** 银行换钱。
- **主要生词：** 想、换、一点儿、钱、办、业务、人民币、稍、等。
- **主要语言点：** 能愿动词“想”，数量词“一点儿”，副词“稍”。
- **文化小常识：** 人民币与汇率。

一 看图讨论 Look at the picture and discuss

1. 他在做什么？ What is he doing?
2. 他会说什么呢？ What might he say?

二 课文 Text

听录音回答问题 Listen to the recording and answer the following questions.

1. 男的想做什么？ What did the man want to do?
2. 女的说了什么？ What did the woman say?

Wǒ xiǎng huàn yìdiǎnr qián
我 想 换 一点儿钱 19-1

gōngzòu rényuán： Nín hǎo! Qǐngwèn nín xiǎng bàn shénme yèwù?
工作 人员：您好！请问您想办什么业务？

Mǎ Wén： Nín hǎo! Wǒ xiǎng huàn yìdiǎnr qián.
马 文：您好！我想换一点儿钱。

gōngzòu rényuán： Nín xiǎng huàn shénme qián ne?
工作 人员：您想换什么钱呢？

Mǎ Wén： Wǒ xiǎng huàn yìdiǎnr rénmínbì.
马 文：我想换一点儿人民币。

gōngzòu rényuán： Hǎo de, qǐng shāo děng.
工作 人员：好的，请稍等。

Mǎ Wén： Xièxie!
马 文：谢谢！

三 生 词 New words 19-2

1.	想	动词	xiǎng	want
2.	换	动词	huàn	change
3.	一点儿	数量词	yìdiǎnr	a little, a bit
4.	钱	名词	qián	money
5.	工作人员		gōngzuò rényuán	staff
6.	办	动词	bàn	do, handle
7.	业务	名词	yèwù	business
8.	人民币	名词	rénmínbì	RMB, Chinese currency
9.	稍	副词	shāo	a little, slightly
10.	等	动词	děng	wait

四 主要语言点 Main language points

1 请问您想办什么业务?

“想”用在动词前边，构成“想 + 动词”的格式，表示愿望、打算或要求。例如：

“想” is used before a verb to form the pattern “想 + V” to express a wish, plan or demand. For example:

（1）弟弟想去公园。
（2）小王想换人民币。
（3）马文想去图书馆。

视频：19.1 我想换一点儿钱。

2 我想换一点儿钱。

数量词“一点儿”用在名词前面，表示数量不多。例如：

The quantifier “一点儿” is used before a noun to indicate a small quantity. For example:

（1）妈妈想换一点儿钱。
（2）我想换一点儿人民币。
（3）爷爷想喝一点儿茶。

视频：19.1 我想换一点儿钱。

3 请稍等！

“请稍等”表示很客气、礼貌地请求别人等一会儿，即等候的时间很短。“稍”是一个副词，用在动词或者形容词前面，表示数量不多或者程度不深。例如：

“请稍等” means to politely ask someone to wait for a while, that is, the waiting time is very short. “稍” is an adverb which is used before a verb or an adjective to indicate a small quantity or low degree. For example:

（1）请稍大（dà）一点儿！
（2）请稍快（kuài）一点儿！

五 文化小常识 General knowledge of culture

人民币与汇率

中国的货币叫作"人民币"，单位有"元、角、分"。中国现在发行的人民币的面额有100元、50元、20元、10元、5元、1元、5角和1角。汇率指不同货币进行兑换时的比率。在中国，各大银行、机场、酒店等地都有外币兑换业务。

RMB and Exchange Rate

The Chinese currency is Renminbi (RMB) and its unit are *yuan*, *jiao* and *fen*. The denominations of RMB currently issued in China include 100 *yuan*, 50 *yuan*, 20 *yuan*, 10 *yuan*, 5 *yuan*, 1 *yuan*, 5 *jiao* and 1 *jiao*. The exchange rate refers to the rate at which currencies of different countries are exchanged. In China, foreign currency exchange service is provided in all major banks, airports, and hotels.

六 练习与实践 Exercises and practice

1 听录音，选择你听到的音，然后朗读下面的拼音。 19-3
Listen to the recording and choose the pronunciation you hear, then read the following Pinyin aloud.

（1）相 — 想 (xiāng xiǎng)　　（2）办 — 班 (bàn bān)　　（3）钱 — 填 (qián tián)

（4）稍（shāo）— 少（shǎo）　（5）灯（dēng）— 等（děng）　（6）还（huán）— 换（huàn）

（7）业务（yèwù）— 延误（yánwù）　（8）人名（rénmíng）— 人民（rénmín）

2 朗读下面的句子，注意语调、语气和重音。

Read the following sentences aloud, paying attention to the tone, intonation and stress.

（1）我想换一点儿钱。

（2）您想换什么钱？

（3）我想换人民币。

（4）好的，请稍等。

3 排列词语成句子。

Arrange the words into sentences.

（1）我　一点儿　换　想　钱

______________________________。

（2）钱　换　想　什么　您

______________________________？

（3）等　稍　请　您

______________________________！

（4）办　您　业务　什么　想

______________________________？

4 用汉语读出下面人民币的面额。

Read the denominations of the following banknotes in Chinese.

（1）＿＿＿＿＿＿＿＿

（2）＿＿＿＿＿＿＿＿

（3）＿＿＿＿＿＿＿＿

（4）＿＿＿＿＿＿＿＿

5 替换练习。

Substitution drills

（1）我想换钱。

去银行
换人民币
去图书馆

（2）我想换一点儿钱。

喝	茶
早	去
买（mǎi）	水（shuǐ）

6 看视频，先填空，然后和同学一起表演视频的内容。

Watch the video and fill in the blanks. Then act out the video with your classmates.

A：您好！请问您______办什么业务？

B：您好！我______换______钱。

视频：19.1 我想换一点儿钱。

7 用汉语给大家介绍一下儿今天人民币和你们国家货币的汇率。

Use Chinese to introduce the exchange rate today between RMB and the currency in your country.

8 汉字练习：看汉字笔画笔顺动态图，并跟着书写。

Practice Chinese characters: Look at the animated illustrations of the strokes and the order of strokes of the following characters, and then write them down.

xiǎng
想

huàn
换

qián
钱

gōng
工

zuò
作

yuán
员

bàn
办

yè
业

wù
务

mín
民

bì
币

shāo
稍

děng
等

第十九课 汉字笔画笔顺动态图

第二十课

Lesson 20

Duōshao qián yí gè
多少钱一个

重点提示

- **交际功能：**买早点。
- **主要生词：**多少、馒头、包子、块、买。
- **主要语言点：**疑问代词“多少”，量词“个、块”，副词“一共”。
- **文化小常识：**中国的早点。

一 看图讨论 Look at the picture and discuss

1. 这些是什么？ What are these?
2. 你知道怎么买吗？ Do you know how to buy them?

二 课文 Text

听录音回答问题 Listen to the recording and answer the following questions.

1. 男的想做什么？他说了些什么？
   What did the man want to do? What did he say?
2. 女的是怎么回答他的？ How did the woman answer him?

Duōshao qián yí gè
多少钱一个 20-1

Mǎ Wén: Nín hǎo, zhèxiē shì shénme?
马 文：您好，这些是什么？

lǎobǎn: Zhèxiē shì mántou, nàxiē shì bāozi.
老 板：这些是馒头，那些是包子。

Mǎ Wén: Duōshao qián yí gè?
马 文：多少钱一个？

lǎobǎn: Mántou yí kuài qián yí gè, bāozi yí kuài wǔ yí gè.
老 板：馒头一块钱一个，包子一块五一个。

Mǎ Wén: Wǒ mǎi wǔ gè mántou、wǔ gè bāozi.
马 文：我买五个馒头、五个包子。

lǎobǎn: Hǎo de, yígòng shí'èr kuài wǔ.
老 板：好的，一共十二块五。

三 生 词 New words 20–2

1.	多少	代词	duōshao	how much, how many
2.	老板	名词	lǎobǎn	shopkeeper
3.	馒头	名词	mántou	steamed bun
4.	包子	名词	bāozi	steamed stuffed bun
5.	块	量词	kuài	*a measure word for money, equivalent to yuan*
6.	买	动词	mǎi	buy
7.	一共	副词	yígòng	altogether

四 主要语言点 Main language points

1 多少钱一个?

"多少"用来询问数量，被问的数量一般在"十"以上，或者是一个难以确定的数量。"多少"后面可以带量词，也可以不带量词。例如：

"多少" is used to ask about a quantity that is usually more than ten or is hard to be determined. "多少" can be followed by a measure word or the measure word can be left out. For example:

（1）你有多少块钱？
（2）你们有多少个人？
（3）学校里有多少老师？

视频：20.1 多少钱一个？

2 馒头一块钱一个，包子一块五一个。

“块”和“个”都是量词，即用来表示人或事物的数量单位，其中“块”是人民币的单位。例如：

Both “块” and “个” are measure words, namely units of measurement for persons or things. “块” is a unit of RMB. For example:

（1）包子两块五一个。
（2）鸡蛋（jīdàn）一块钱一个。
（3）面包（miànbāo）三块五毛钱一个。

“个”做量词时的使用范围比较广，可以用作人的量词，也可以用作物的量词。用来交际时的口语性很强，表达比较随意。例如：

As a measure word, “个” is widely used. It can be used as a measure word for both persons and things. It is very colloquial in communication, and is a rather casual expression. For example:

（1）我们有二十个同学。
（2）我买三个包子。
（3）他买一个馒头。

视频： 20.1 多少钱一个？

3 一共十二块五。

“一共”是一个副词，表示某个范围内的人或事物合在一起的总数量。例如：

“一共” is an adverb, indicating the total quantity of people or things in a certain range. For example:

（1）我们学校一共有三百人。
（2）馒头、包子一共五块钱。
（3）这课一共有十五个生词（shēngcí）。

五 文化小常识 General knowledge of culture

中国的早点

早点，又叫早餐，是中国人早上吃的食物的统称。中国各地有着丰富多样的早点，代表着不同地域的文化和不同地区人群的生活习惯。其中，馒头、包子、油条、豆浆、鸡蛋和面条儿等是全国各地最常见的早点。中国的早点美味可口，营养健康，很多外国朋友也都很喜欢吃。

Chinese Breakfast

"早点", also called "早餐", is a collective term for food that Chinese people eat in the morning. There are rich varieties of breakfast foods in various places of China, which represent the culture of different places and the living habits of people in different regions. Among them, steamed buns, steamed stuffed buns, soybean milk, eggs and noodles are the most common breakfast foods all over the country. Chinese breakfast is delicious, nutritious and healthy. Many foreign friends also like them very much.

六 练习与实践 Exercises and practice

1 听录音，选择你听到的音，然后朗读下面的拼音。 20–3
Listen to the recording and choose the pronunciation you hear, then read the following Pinyin aloud.

mǎi　mán	bāo　dāo	gòng　kōng
(1) 买 — 馒	(2) 包 — 刀	(3) 共 — 空

mán máng
(4) 馒 — 忙

zǐ zhǐ
(5) 子 — 指

qián xián
(6) 钱 — 咸

mántou mànzǒu
(7) 馒头 — 慢走

duōshao dōu xiǎo
(8) 多少 — 都 小

2 朗读下面的句子，注意语调、语气和重音。

Read the following sentences aloud, paying attention to the tone, intonation and stress.

(1) 这是什么？

(2) 包子多少钱一个？

(3) 包子一块五一个。

(4) 我买五个馒头、五个包子。

(5) 好的，一共十二块五。

3 排列词语成句子。

Arrange the words into sentences.

(1) 什么　那些　是

______________________________？

(2) 是　馒头　那些

______________________________。

(3) 钱　多少　个　一

______________________________？

(4) 馒头　一个　一块五

______________________________。

（5）馒头　五　个　买　我

________________。

4 替换练习：先替换画线的部分，然后和同学一起模仿对话。
Substitution drills: Replace the underlined parts first, then imitate the following dialogue with your classmates.

A：馒头多少钱一个？
B：一块钱一个。
A：我买五个。

包子	一块五毛	六个
面包	两块五毛	三个
鸡蛋	两块	四个

5 看图完成下面的对话，然后和同学一起演示一下儿对话的内容。
Look at the picture and complete the following dialogue, then act it out with your classmates.

A：包子______钱一______？
B：一______五一______。
A：我买五______。
B：好的，______七______五。

❻ 介绍一下儿你自己国家的早餐或者你爱吃的中国早餐。
Introduce the breakfast in your country or your favorite Chinese breakfast food.

❼ 汉字练习：看汉字笔画笔顺动态图，并跟着书写。
Practice Chinese characters: Look at the animated illustrations of the strokes and the order of strokes of the following characters, and then write them down.

shao
少

bǎn
板

mán
馒

tou
头

bāo
包

zi
子

mǎi
买

gòng
共

èr
二

kuài
块

第二十课 汉字笔画笔顺动态图

第二十一课
Lesson 21

Nǐ zài wǎng shang gòuwù ma
你在网上购物吗

重点提示

- **交际功能：** 网上购物。
- **主要生词：** 网上、购物、方便、商品、质量、怎么样、有的。
- **主要语言点：** 在……上，疑问代词“怎么样”，有的……有的……
- **文化小常识：** 网购简介。

一 看图讨论 Look at the picture and discuss

1. 他们在做什么？ What are they doing?
2. 他们会说什么呢？ What might they say?

二 课文 Text

听录音回答问题 Listen to the recording and answer the following questions.

1. 马文问了什么？ What did Ma Wen ask?
2. 李安平回答了些什么？ What did Li Anping answer?

Nǐ zài wǎng shang gòuwù ma
你在网上购物吗 21-1

Mǎ Wén: Nǐ zài wǎng shang gòuwù ma?
马文：你在网上购物吗？

Lǐ Ānpíng: Shì a, wǎnggòu hěn fāngbiàn.
李安平：是啊，网购很方便。

Mǎ Wén: Wǎng shang de shāngpǐn duō ma?
马文：网上的商品多吗？

Lǐ Ānpíng: Hěn duō.
李安平：很多。

Mǎ Wén: Shāngpǐn de zhìliàng zěnmeyàng?
马文：商品的质量怎么样？

Lǐ Ānpíng: Yǒude hěn hǎo, yǒude bù hǎo.
李安平：有的很好，有的不好。

三 生词 New words 21-2

1.	网上		wǎng shang	online, on the Internet
2.	购物	动词	gòuwù	go shopping
3.	啊	语气词	a	*a modal particle used at the end of a sentence to indicate agreement, etc.*
4.	网购	动词	wǎnggòu	shop online
5.	方便	形容词	fāngbiàn	convenient
6.	商品	名词	shāngpǐn	commodity
7.	质量	名词	zhìliàng	quality
8.	怎么样	代词	zěnmeyàng	how, how about
9.	有的	代词	yǒude	some

四 主要语言点 Main language points

1 你在网上购物吗？

这个句子中的"在"是一个介词，用于"在 + 名词 / 名词短语 + 上 / 里 + 动词"的格式中，表示动作或行为发生的位置。例如：

"在" in this sentence is a preposition used in the structure "在 + N/NP + 上/里 + V" to indicate where an action or behavior occurs. For example:

（1）我在网上购物。
（2）老师在网上上课。
（3）她在图书馆里看（kàn）书。

视频：21.1 你在网上购物吗？

2 商品的质量怎么样？

这个句子中的“怎么样”是一个疑问代词，用来询问对方对某人、某事或某物的看法及评价。例如：

“怎么样” in this sentence is an interrogative pronoun used to ask the other party's opinions or comments on somebody or something. For example:

（1）网上的商品怎么样？

（2）学校的包子怎么样？

（3）这里（zhèli）的馒头怎么样？

视频：21.2 商品的质量怎么样？

3 有的很好，有的不好。

“有的”是一个代词，用来指代某个整体中的一部分，可以单用，也可以两个或三个连用。例如：

“有的” is a pronoun used to refer to a part of a whole. It can either be used independently or together in twos or threes. For example:

（1）网上的商品有的很好。

（2）这些书有的很好，有的不好。

（3）同学们有的是泰国人，有的是美国人，有的是英国（Yīngguó）人。

视频：21.2 商品的质量怎么样？

五 文化小常识 General knowledge of culture

网购简介

“网购”是“网上购物”的简称。人们首先在购物网站上选好自己想买的物品，网上付款后，网站上的卖家就会通过快递送货到家。网购的物品一般在 7 天内可以无理由退货。网上购物已经成为很多中国人的主要购物方式。2022 年，中国的网上零售额达 13.79 万亿元，跨境电商进出口总额达 2.11 万亿元。

Brief Introduction to Online Shopping

“网购” is the abbreviation of “网上购物 (online shopping)”. People choose the items they want to buy on the shopping website first. Then, after they pay online, the sellers on the website deliver the items to them by express delivery. Items purchased online can generally be returned without a reason within 7 days. Online shopping has become a main way of shopping for many Chinese people. In 2022, the number of China’s online retail sales had reached 13.79 trillion *yuan*, and China’s cross-border online shopping volume reached 2.11 trillion *yuan*.

六 练习与实践 Exercises and practice

1 听录音，选择你听到的音，然后朗读下面的拼音。 21-3

Listen to the recording and choose the pronunciation you hear, then read the following Pinyin aloud.

wǎng wáng （1）网 — 王	hòu gòu （2）后 — 购	wù mù （3）物 — 木
yòu yǒu （4）又 — 有	fàn fāng （5）饭 — 方	shān shāng （6）山 — 商
píng pǐn （7）平 — 品	zhì jì （8）质 — 记	yàng liàng （9）样 — 量
wǎng shang wǎnshang （10）网 上 — 晚上	gēwǔ gòuwù （11）歌舞 — 购物	
fǎnmiàn fāngbiàn （12）反面 — 方便	zhìliàng jǐ yàng （13）质量 — 几 样	

2 朗读下面的句子，注意语调、语气和重音。

Read the following sentences aloud, paying attention to the tone, intonation and stress.

（1）你在网上购物吗？
（2）这些包子怎么样？
（3）网上购物方便吗？
（4）商品的质量有的很好，有的不好。
（5）网购很方便。

3 排列词语成句子。

Arrange the words into sentences.

（1）怎么样　这些　质量　的　商品

______________________________？

（2）的　商品　网上　有的　有的　很好　不好

____。

（3）在　你　网上　吗　购物

____？

（4）上课　很　网上　方便　在

____。

4 选词填空。
Choose the words to fill in the blanks.

怎么样　网购　商品　方便　网上　有的……有的……

（1）我们在________看书。

（2）很多人喜欢（xǐhuan）________。

（3）________的质量________？

（4）在网上学汉语很________。

（5）这课的生词________很难（nán），________不难。

5 替换练习。
Substitution drills

（1）我在<u>网上</u><u>购物</u>。

飞机（fēijī）	看书
地铁	打电话（dǎ diànhuà）
书	写字（xiě zì）

（2）网上商品的质量怎么样？

这些书
那种手机
网上教学（jiàoxué）

6 看图完成下面的对话，然后和同学一起演示一下儿对话的内容。
Look at the picture and complete the following dialogue, then act it out with your classmates.

A：你在做什么？

B：我在________购物。

A：________商品的质量________？

B：________很好，________不好。

7 说说你的国家的购物网站和上面商品的质量，注意用上下面的词语。
Talk about the shopping websites in your country and the quality of the commodities on the websites. Use the following words.

网购　　质量　　商品　　方便　　网上　　有的……有的……

8 看视频，先回答问题，然后说说你对网购的看法。
Watch the video and answer the questions. Then talk about your views on online shopping.

（1）男生问了什么？
（2）女生回答了什么？

视频：21.2 商品的质量怎么样？

9 汉字练习：看汉字笔画笔顺动态图，并跟着书写。
Practice Chinese characters: Look at the animated illustrations of the strokes and the order of strokes of the following characters, and then write them down.

wǎng
网

gòu
购

wù
物

a
啊

fāng
方

biàn
便

shāng
商

pǐn
品

zhì
质

liàng
量

yàng
样

第二十一课　汉字笔画笔顺动态图

综合实践二

第二十二课
Lesson 22

Guóqìng Jié shì jǐ yuè jǐ hào
国庆节是几月几号

重点提示

- **交际功能：** 谈论节日的日期。
- **主要生词：** 国庆节、中秋节、时候、说、日期。
- **主要语言点：** 用“什么时候”询问时间。
- **文化小常识：** 国庆节简介。

一 看图讨论 Look at the picture and discuss

1. 你知道下面的图片是中国的哪个节日吗？这个节日是哪天呢？
   Do you know which Chinese festival is shown in the following picture? What day is the festival?
2. 你们国家的这个节日是哪天呢？ What day is this festival in your country?

二 课文 Text

听录音回答问题 Listen to the recording and answer the following questions.

1. 他们说到了哪些节日？ What festivals did they talk about?
2. 你知道这些节日的日期吗？ Do you know the dates of these festivals?

Guóqìng Jié shì jǐ yuè jǐ hào
国庆节是几月几号 22-1

Mǎ Wén: Zhōngguó de Guóqìng Jié shì jǐ yuè jǐ hào?
马 文： 中国 的 国庆 节是几月几号？

Lǐ Ānpíng: Shí yuè yī hào.
李 安平： 十 月一号。

Mǎ Wén: Zhōngguó de Zhōngqiū Jié shì jǐ yuè jǐ hào?
马 文： 中国 的 中秋 节是几月几号？

Lǐ Ānpíng: Shì nónglì bā yuè shíwǔ, bù shuō "hào".
李 安平： 是农历八月 十五，不 说 "号"。

Mǎ Wén: Nà shénme shíhou shuō "hào", shénme shíhou bù shuō "hào" ne?
马 文： 那什么 时候 说"号"，什么 时候不 说"号"呢？

Lǐ Ānpíng: Gōnglì de rìqī shuō "hào", nónglì de rìqī bù shuō "hào".
李 安平： 公历的日期说 "号"，农历的日期不 说 "号"。

三 生 词 New words 22-2

1.	国庆节	专有名词	Guóqìng Jié	National Day
2.	中秋节	专有名词	Zhōngqiū Jié	Mid-Autumn Festival
3.	时候	名词	shíhou	time, moment
4.	说	动词	shuō	say
5.	日期	名词	rìqī	date

四 主要语言点 Main language points

那什么时候说“号”？

“什么时候”可用来询问某个特定的时刻或者某一特定的时间段，由疑问代词“什么”与名词“时候”组合而成，常用在动词前面。例如：

“什么时候” is used to ask about a specific point in time or a specific period of time. It is made up of the interrogative pronoun “什么” and the noun “时候” and is often used before a verb. For example:

（1）你什么时候去图书馆？

（2）我们什么时候考试？

（3）你什么时候去中国？

（4）什么时候说“你”，什么时候说“您”呢？

视频：22.1 那什么时候说“号”？

五 文化小常识 General knowledge of culture

国庆节

国庆节是一个国家纪念国家独立或者元首出生等重大事件的周年纪念日，是每个国家的重要节日。各国在国庆节这一天都要举行不同形式的庆祝活动。中华人民共和国，简称中国，成立于1949年10月1日，因此，中国的国庆节是公历的10月1日。泰国的国庆节是12月5日。越南的国庆节是9月2日。老挝的国庆日是12月2日。印度尼西亚的国庆节是8月17日。

National Day

The National Day is the anniversary of a major national event, such as national independence or the birth of a head of the state. It is an important festival for each country. All countries hold different forms of celebration on their national day. The People's Republic of China, or China for short, was founded on October 1, 1949. Therefore, China's National Day falls on October 1 of the Gregorian calendar. Thailand's National Day is December 5. Vietnam's National Day is September 2. Laos' National Day is December 2. Indonesia's National Day is August 17.

六 练习与实践 Exercises and practice

1 听录音，选择你听到的音，然后朗读下面的拼音。22-3
Listen to the recording and choose the pronunciation you hear, then read the following Pinyin aloud.

guǒ guó （1）果 — 国	qìng jìn （2）庆 — 近	jié xiě （3）节 — 写
jiù qiū （4）就 — 秋	shùn chūn （5）顺 — 春	shuō zhuō （6）说 — 捉
Zhōngguó chónghuò （7）中国 — 重获	guòjìng guóqìng （8）过境 — 国庆	
chóngxiū Zhōngqiū （9）重修 — 中秋	rìqī ěrjī （10）日期 — 耳机	

2 朗读下面的句子，注意语调、语气和重音。
Read the following sentences aloud, paying attention to the tone, intonation and stress.

（1）中国的端午节是几月几号？
（2）公历十月一号是中国的国庆节。
（3）我们什么时候去图书馆？
（4）中国的中秋节是农历八月十五。
（5）什么时候不说“号”呢？

3 排列词语成句子。
Arrange the words into sentences.

（1）端午节　五月　农历　初五　中国　的　是

____。

（2）中国　什么　教师节　是　的　时候

____？

（3）中秋节　是　中国　八月　的　农历　十五。

____。

（4）几　国庆节　几　的　公历　中国　月　是　号

____？

4 替换练习。
Substitution drills

（1）中国的国庆节是十月一号。

教师节（Jiàoshī Jié）	九月十号
劳动节（Láodòng Jié）	五月一号
儿童节（Értóng Jié）	六月一号

（2）端午节是农历五月初五。

中秋节	八月十五
春节（Chūnjié）	正月（zhēngyuè）初一
元宵节（Yuánxiāo Jié）	正月十五

5 看图完成下面的对话，然后和同学一起演示一下儿对话的内容。
Look at the pictures and complete the following dialogues, then act out the dialogues with your classmates.

（1）A：中国的中秋节是__________？

B：中国的中秋节是农历__________。

（2）A：中国的春节是__________？

B：中国的春节是农历__________。

6 介绍一下儿世界上或者你们国家一些重要节日的日期，注意用上下面的词语。

Introduce the dates of some important festivals in the world or in your own country. Use the following words.

日期　　国庆节　　节　　公历　　几月　　几号

7 看视频，先回答问题，然后给朋友介绍一下儿这些节日的日期。

Watch the video and answer the questions. Then introduce the dates of these festivals to your friends.

（1）中国的国庆节是什么时候？是公历还是农历？

（2）中国的中秋节是什么时候？是公历还是农历？

（3）什么时候说"号"，什么时候不说"号"？

视频：22.2 国庆节是几月几号？

8 汉字练习：看汉字笔画笔顺动态图，并跟着书写。

Practice Chinese characters: Look at the animated illustrations of the strokes and the order of strokes of the following characters, and then write them down.

qìng
庆

qiū
秋

shí
时

hou
候

shuō
说

第二十二课　汉字笔画笔顺动态图

第二十三课

Lesson

23

Qù jīchǎng zěnme zǒu

去机场怎么走

重点提示

- **交际功能：**询问和介绍交通路线。
- **主要生词：**北边、坐、先、然后、转、下车。
- **主要语言点：**连动句，先……然后……。
- **文化小常识：**广州地铁。

一 看图讨论 Look at the picture and discuss

1. 他们准备去哪儿？ Where are they going?
2. 他们将怎么去呢？ How will they go there?

二 课文 Text

听录音回答问题 Listen to the recording and answer the questions.

1. 机场在哪儿？ Where is the airport?
2. 他们打算怎么去呢？ How will they go there?

Qù jīchǎng zěnme zǒu
去机场怎么走 23-1

Mǎ Wén: Jīchǎng zài nǎr?
马 文：机场 在 哪儿？

Lǐ Ānpíng: Zài Guǎngzhōu de běibian.
李 安平：在 广州 的 北边。

Mǎ Wén: Wǒmen zěnme qù jīchǎng ne?
马 文：我们 怎么去机场呢？

Lǐ Ānpíng: Wǒmen zuò dìtiě qù.
李 安平：我们 坐 地铁 去。

Mǎ Wén: Zěnme zuò ne?
马 文：怎么 坐 呢？

Lǐ Ānpíng: Xiān zuò yī hào xiàn, ránhòu zhuǎn èr hào xiàn, zài zhōngdiǎn zhàn xià chē.
李 安平：先 坐 一 号 线，然后 转 二 号 线，在 终点 站 下 车。

Mǎ Wén: Hǎo de.
马 文：好 的。

三 生词 New words 23-2

1.	机场	名词	jīchǎng	airport
2.	广州	专有名词	Guǎngzhōu	Guangzhou
2.	北边	名词	běibian	north (side)
3.	坐	动词	zuò	travel by (bus, train, plane, etc.)
4.	先	副词	xiān	first, at the beginning
5.	一号线		yī hào xiàn	Line 1
	号	量词	hào	*a measure word indicating order*
	线	名词	xiàn	route, line
6.	然后	副词	ránhòu	then
7.	转	动词	zhuǎn	transfer
8.	终点站		zhōngdiǎn zhàn	terminal
9.	下车		xià chē	get off (the train)

四 主要语言点 Main language points

1 我们坐地铁去。

这个句子中的“坐”和“去”都是“我们”发出的动作行为，这种谓语由两个或两个以上的动词或动词短语组成的句子叫连动句。这种句子可以表示动作的方式。例如：

Both the actions of “坐” and “去” in this sentence are what “we” did. A sentence in which the predicate is made up of two or more verbs or verb phrases is known as a sentence with serial verbs. This type of sentence can indicate the way to do something. For example:

（1）我们坐出租车（chūzūchē）去学校。

（2）我们坐地铁去机场。

（3）爸爸坐飞机去中国。

视频：23.1 坐地铁去机场。

2 先坐一号线，然后转二号线，在终点站下车。

“先……，然后……”表示两个动作在时间上的先后顺序。例如：

“先……, 然后……” is used to indicate the time sequence of two actions. For example:

（1）我们先上课，然后去图书馆。

（2）妈妈先去银行，然后去学校。

（3）你先坐三号线，然后转五号线，在终点站下车。

视频：23.1 坐地铁去机场。

五 文化小常识 General knowledge of culture

广州地铁

广州地铁是中国广东省广州市的城市地下铁路交通系统。2022 年，广州地铁的运营线路共 16 条，总长 621 公里。广州市的机场、高铁站、火车站等都有地铁线路到达。广州地铁已经成为广大市民出行的主要交通工具之一。2023 年，广州地铁线路总长将超过 800 公里。

Guangzhou Metro

Guangzhou metro is the urban underground railway transportation system in Guangzhou, Guangdong Province, China. In 2022, there were 16 operating metro lines in Guangzhou, with a total length of 621 kilometers. There are metro lines to the airport, high-speed railway stations and railway stations in Guangzhou. Guangzhou metro has become one of the main means of transportation for the general public. En 2023, the total length of Guangzhou metro lines will exceed 800 kilometers.

六 练习与实践 Exercises and practice

1 听录音，选择你听到的音，然后朗读下面的拼音。23-3
Listen to the recording and choose the pronunciation you hear, then read the following Pinyin aloud.

(1) 机 jī — 起 qǐ
(2) 坐 zuò — 错 cuò
(3) 转 zhuǎn — 传 chuán
(4) 先 xiān — 前 qián
(5) 然 rān — 年 nián
(6) 终 zhōng — 总 zǒng
(7) 机场 jīchǎng — 细长 xìcháng
(8) 下车 xià chē — 叫车 jiào chē
(9) 然后 ránhòu — 年后 nián hòu
(10) 终点 zhōngdiǎn — 从前 cóngqián

2 朗读下面的句子，注意语调、语气和重音。
Read the following sentences aloud, paying attention to the tone, intonation and stress.

(1) 地铁站在哪儿？
(2) 我们怎么去机场？
(3) 去中国银行怎么走？
(4) 我们坐飞机去北京。
(5) 先坐一号线，然后转二号线，在终点站下车。

3 排列词语成句子。
Arrange the words into sentences.

(1) 哪儿　地铁站　在

____________________________________？

（2）机场　呢　我们　去　怎么

______________________________？

（3）哪儿　呢　我们　去　地铁　坐

______________________________？

（4）四号线　然后　坐　先　三号线　转

______________________________。

4 替换练习：先替换画线的部分，然后和同学一起模仿对话。

Substitution drills: Replace the underlined parts first, then imitate the following dialogue with your classmates.

A：我们怎么去<u>机场</u>呢？
B：我们坐<u>地铁</u>去。

学校	出租车（chūzūchē）
银行	公交车（gōngjiāochē）
中国	飞机（fēijī）

5 完成对话，然后和同学演示对话的内容。

Complete the dialogue, and then act it out with your classmates.

A：我们________去广州南站（Guǎngzhōunán Zhàn）？

B：我们________地铁________广州南站。

A：我们________坐呢？

B：________坐一号线，________转二号线，在________站下车。

6 看视频，先回答问题，然后和同学一起表演视频的内容。

Watch the video and answer the questions. Then act out the video with your classmates.

（1）他们打算怎么去机场？

（2）他们去机场的时候怎么坐地铁？

（3）他们在哪儿下地铁？

视频：23.1 坐地铁去机场。

7 介绍一下儿自己去机场的出行方式和路线，注意用上下面的词语。

Describe your travel mode and route to the airport. Use the following words.

去　　机场　　坐　　转　　终点站　　地铁

8 汉字练习：看汉字笔画笔顺动态图，并跟着书写。

Practice Chinese characters: Look at the animated illustrations of the strokes and the order of strokes of the following characters, and then write them down.

chǎng
场

guǎng
广

zhōu
州

běi
北

zuò
坐

xiān
先

xiàn
线

rán
然

hòu
后

zhuǎn
转

zhōng
终

第二十三课　汉字笔画笔顺动态图

第二十四课

Lesson 24

Píngguǒ duōshao qián yì jīn

苹果多少钱一斤

重点提示

- **交际功能**：购物讲价。
- **主要生词**：斤、大、小、两、收、找。
- **主要语言点**："形容词＋的"结构，用"怎么样"表示询问。
- **文化小常识**：汉语的重量单位"斤"。

一 看图讨论 Look at the picture and discuss

1. 女的在做什么？她会问什么？ What is the woman doing? What might she ask?
2. 男的会怎么回答？ How might the man answer her?

二 课 文 Text

听录音回答问题 Listen to the recording and answer the questions.

1. 马文在做什么？他问了什么？ What is Ma Wen doing? What did he ask?
2. 女的是怎么回答的？ How did the woman answer him?

Píngguǒ duōshao qián yì jīn
苹果 多少 钱 一 斤 24-1

Mǎ Wén: Nín hǎo, qǐngwèn píngguǒ duōshao qián yì jīn?
马 文：您 好，请问 苹果 多少 钱一斤？

lǎobǎn: Dàde shíyī kuài wǔ, xiǎode liù kuài.
老板：大的十一 块 五，小的六块。

Mǎ Wén: Dàde piányi yìdiǎnr, zěnmeyàng?
马 文：大的 便宜 一点儿，怎么样？

lǎobǎn: Nín mǎi duōshao?
老板：您 买 多少？

Mǎ Wén: Wǒ mǎi liǎng jīn.
马 文：我 买 两 斤。

lǎobǎn: Nà shí kuài yì jīn, yígòng èrshí kuài, zěnmeyàng?
老板：那十 块一斤，一共二十块，怎么样？

Mǎ Wén: Hǎo de.
马 文：好 的。

lǎobǎn: Shōu nín wǔshí kuài, zhǎo nín sānshí kuài.
老板：收 您 五十块，找 您 三十块。

三 生词 New words 24-2

1.	苹果	名词	píngguǒ	apple
2.	斤	量词	jīn	*a measure word for weight, equivalent to 0.5 kilograms*
3.	大	形容词	dà	big
4.	小	形容词	xiǎo	small
5.	便宜	形容词	piányi	cheap, inexpensive
6.	两	数词	liǎng	two
7.	收	动词	shōu	receive
8.	找	动词	zhǎo	give change

四 主要语言点 Main language points

1 大的十一块五，小的六块。

"大的""小的"是由"形容词＋的"构成的"的"字短语，其功能相当于一个名词。这种表达可以避免重复，例如：

"大的" and "小的" are 的-phrases composed of "adjective + 的" and are used as nouns. Such an expression can avoid repetition. For example:

（1）包子大的两块，小的一块。
（2）苹果大的贵（guì），小的便宜。
（3）这两个学生，大的是哥哥，小的是弟弟。

视频：24.1 苹果多少钱一斤？

2 大的便宜一点儿，怎么样？

“怎么样”用在句尾，构成“……，怎么样”这样的问句，用来表示客气地向对方征询意见。如果同意，对方回答时常常说“好”或者“好的”。例如：

“怎么样” is used at the end of a sentence to form the question “……，怎么样”. It is used to politely ask for the other party’s opinion. The other party often says “好” or “好的” if he agrees. For example:

（1）A：我们坐地铁去机场，怎么样？
B：好。/ 好的。
（2）A：我们八点去图书馆，怎么样？
B：好。/ 好的。
（3）A：苹果便宜一点儿，怎么样？
B：好。/ 好的。

视频：24.1 苹果多少钱一斤？

五 文化小常识 General knowledge of culture

汉语的重量单位“斤”

“斤”原是中国古代的重量单位，现在中国人在日常生活中也常用。中国人常用的重量单位还有“两”。不过，中国古代的“斤、两”和现在的“斤、两”有点儿不同。古代一斤等于十六两，半斤等于八两，因此有“半斤八两”这一成语。现在的一斤等于十两，半斤等于五两。一斤等于五百克，一两等于五十克，两斤等于一公斤。

The Chinese Unit of Weight *Jin*

Jin was a unit of weight in ancient China, and it is also commonly used in Chinese people's daily life today. Another common unit of weight that Chinese people use is *liang*. However, *jin* and *liang* in ancient times are slightly different from those at present. In ancient times, one *jin* equals sixteen *liang*, and half a *jin* equals eight *liang*, hence the idiom *banjinbaliang* (meaning "half a *jin* equals eight *liang*, much of a muchness"). At present, one *jin* equals ten *liang*, and half *jin* equals five *liang*. One *jin* equals 500 grams, one *liang* equals 50 grams, and two *jin* equals one kilogram.

六 练习与实践 Exercises and practice

1 听录音，选择你听到的音，然后朗读下面的拼音。 24-3
Listen to the recording and choose the pronunciation you hear, then read the following Pinyin aloud.

zǎo zhǎo （1）早 — 找	jīn qīn （2）斤 — 亲	pīn píng （3）拼 — 苹
dà tā （4）大 — 他	shōu zhōu （5）收 — 周	biān pián （6）边 — 便
zhǒng zǒng （7）种 — 总	shì sì （8）是 — 四	gòng kòng （9）共 — 空

2 朗读下面的句子，注意语调、语气和重音。

Read the following sentences aloud, paying attention to the tone, intonation and stress.

（1）大的十一块五，小的六块。

（2）大的便宜一点儿，怎么样？

（3）你买多少？

（4）那十块一斤，一共二十块，怎么样？

3 用汉语的词语"斤"说出下面水果的重量。

Use the Chinese word "斤" to tell the weight of the following fruits.

（1）2.5 kg =______斤

（2）1.25 kg =______斤

（3）1.1 kg =______斤

（4）0.8 kg =______斤

4 用汉语说出下面物品的价格。
Use Chinese to tell the prices of the following items.

（1）______元一斤

（2）______元一个

（3）______元一个

（4）______元一个

5 替换练习：先替换画线的部分，然后和同学一起模仿对话。
Substitution drills: Replace the underlined parts first, then imitate the following dialogue with your classmates.

A：请问苹果多少钱一斤？
B：十二块钱一斤，你买多少？

包子	个
橙子（chéngzi）	斤
香蕉（xiāngjiāo）	斤

两块五一个
五块五一斤
六块钱一斤

A：我买三斤。

B：一共三十六块。

十个
五斤
两斤

二十五块
二十七块五
十二块

6 看图完成下面的对话，然后和同学一起演示一下儿对话的内容。

Look at the picture and complete the following dialogue, then act it out with your classmates.

A：书__________钱一本（běn）？

B：四十二块钱一本。

A：便宜__________，__________？

B：那四十块钱一本吧。

A：__________，谢谢！

7 介绍一下儿现在市场上苹果、香蕉等水果的价格，注意用上下面的词语。

Introduce the prices of apples, bananas, and other fruits on the market. Use the following words.

斤　　块　　便宜　　一点儿　　大的　　小的

8 看视频，先填空。然后和同学一起表演视频的内容。

Watch the video and fill in the blanks. Then act out the video with your classmates.

A：你好，苹果________钱一斤？

B：________十一块五________，________六块五________。

A：________便宜一点儿，________？

视频：24.1苹果多少钱一斤？

9 汉字练习：看汉字笔画笔顺动态图，并跟着书写。

Practice Chinese characters: Look at the animated illustrations of the strokes and the order of strokes of the following characters, and then write them down.

píng
苹

guǒ
果

jīn
斤

dà
大

xiǎo
小

pián
便

yi
宜

liǎng
两

shōu
收

zhǎo
找

第二十四课 汉字笔画笔顺动态图

生词表

A	啊	语气词	a	*a modal particle used at the end of a sentence to indicate agreement, etc.*	21
B	八	数词	bā	eight	13
	爸爸	名词	bàba	father, dad	4
	百	数词	bǎi	hundred	18
	办	动词	bàn	do, handle	19
	半	数词	bàn	half	13
	包子	名词	bāozi	steamed stuffed bun	20
	北边	名词	běibian	north (side)	23
	不客气		bú kèqi	you are welcome	9
	不	副词	bù	not	11
C	初五		chū wǔ	the fifth day of a lunar month	15
D	大	形容词	dà	big	24
	地铁	名词	dìtiě	subway, metro	17
	地铁站	名词	dìtiězhàn	subway station	17
	的	助词	de	*used after an attribute to indicate possession*	4
	等	动词	děng	wait	19
	点	量词	diǎn	o'clock	13
	东边	名词	dōngbian	east (side)	18
	东门		dōng mén	east gate	18

	都	副词	dōu	all, both	12
	端午节	专有名词	Duānwǔ Jié	Dragon Boat Festival	15
	多	形容词	duō	more	8
	多少	代词	duōshao	how much, how many	20
F	方便	形容词	fāngbiàn	convenient	21
	分	量词	fēn	minute	13
	附近	名词	fùjìn	nearby	18
G	个	量词	gè	*a measure word used before nouns without a particular measure word of their own*	14
	工作人员		gōngzuò rényuán	staff	19
	公历	名词	gōnglì	Gregorian calendar	15
	购物	动词	gòuwù	go shopping	21
	拐	动词	guǎi	turn, change direction	18
	广州	专有名词	Guǎngzhōu	Guangzhou	23
	贵姓	名词	guìxìng	*an honorific expression for asking the other party's family name*	10
	国	名词	guó	country	11
	国家	名词	guójiā	country	9
	国庆节	专有名词	Guóqìng Jié	National Day	22
H	好	形容词	hǎo	fine, good	1
	号	名词	hào	*referring to a date of a month*	15
	号	量词	hào	*a measure word indicating order*	23
	很	副词	hěn	very	3

欢迎	动词	huānyíng	welcome	9
换	动词	huàn	change	19

J

机场	名词	jīchǎng	airport	23
几	代词	jǐ	what, how many	13
见	名词	jiàn	see	7
江山	专有名词	Jiāng Shān	Jiang Shan, a person's name	10
叫	动词	jiào	call, be called	10
教学楼	名词	jiàoxuélóu	teaching building	16
节	名词	jié	festival	15
斤	量词	jīn	a measure word for weight, equivalent to 0.5 kilograms	24
今天	名词	jīntiān	today	14

K

考试	动词	kǎoshì	have an examination	14
课本	名词	kèběn	textbook	12
块	量词	kuài	*a measure word for money, equivalent to yuan*	20

L

老板	名词	lǎobǎn	shopkeeper	20
老师	名词	lǎoshī	teacher	2
李安平	专有名词	Lǐ Ānpíng	Li Anping, a person's name	1
联系	动词	liánxì	contact	8
两	数词	liǎng	two	24
留步	动词	liúbù	(*a polite remark made to a host when a guest leaves*) don't bother to see me out	8
路	名词	lù	road	7

	路人	名词	lùrén	passer-by	16
	路上	名词	lùshang	on the road	7
M	妈妈	名词	māma	mother, mom	4
	马文	专有名词	Mǎ Wén	Ma Wen, a person's name	1
	吗	助词	ma	*a particle used at the end of a yes/no question*	3
	买	动词	mǎi	buy	20
	馒头	名词	mántou	steamed bun	20
	慢走	动词	mànzǒu	(at parting) goodbye, take care	8
	没有	动词	méiyǒu	not have	6
	美国	专有名词	Měiguó	the United States	11
	美国人	专有名词	Měiguórén	American (people)	11
	们	后缀	men	*a suffix used to indicate the plural*	2
	米	量词	mǐ	meter	18
	免	动词	miǎn	don't have to...	10
	明天	名词	míngtiān	tomorrow	14
N	哪	代词	nǎ	which	11
	哪儿	代词	nǎr	where	16
	那	代词	nà	that	5
	那	连词	nà	that	6
	那边	代词	nàbiān	over there	17
	那些	代词	nàxiē	those	12
	男	名词	nán	man	8
	呢	助词	ne	*a particle used at the end of a question*	5
	你	代词	nǐ	you	1

	你好		nǐ hǎo	hello, hi	1
	你们	代词	nǐmen	you (*plural*)	2
	您	代词	nín	you (*honorific*)	10
	农历	名词	nónglì	lunar calendar	15
	女	名词	nǚ	woman	8
	女儿	名词	nǚ'er	daughter	7
P	旁边	名词	pángbiān	beside	17
	便宜	形容词	piányi	cheap, inexpensive	24
	平安	形容词	píng'ān	safe and sound	9
	苹果	名词	píngguǒ	apple	24
Q	前面	名词	qiánmiàn	front	16
	钱	名词	qián	money	19
	请	动词	qǐng	please	8
	请问	动词	qǐngwèn	*an honorific expression used to ask the other party to answer a question*	10
	去	动词	qù	go	9
R	然后	副词	ránhòu	then	23
	人	名词	rén	person, people	11
	人民币	名词	rénmínbì	RMB, Chinese currency	19
	日期	名词	rìqī	date	22
S	商品	名词	shāngpǐn	commodity	21
	上课	动词	shàngkè	start class	13
	上	名词	shang	*used after a noun to indicate the scope of something*	7
	稍	副词	shāo	a little, slightly	19

	谁	代词	shéi	who	4
	什么	代词	shénme	what	5
	生日	名词	shēngrì	birthday	15
	十	数词	shí	ten	13
	时候	名词	shíhou	time, moment	22
	是	动词	shì	is, am, are	1
	收	动词	shōu	receive	24
	手机	名词	shǒujī	mobile phone	5
	书	名词	shū	book	5
	说	动词	shuō	say	22
T	他	代词	tā	he, him	4
	她	代词	tā	she, her	4
	泰国	专有名词	Tàiguó	Thailand	11
	泰国人	专有名词	Tàiguórén	Thai (people)	11
	同学	名词	tóngxué	classmate	12
	图书馆	名词	túshūguǎn	library	16
W	晚上	名词	wǎnshang	evening, night	7
	王老师		Wáng lǎoshī	Mr./Ms. Wang	2
	王云平	专有名词	Wáng Yúnpíng	Wang Yunping, a person's name	10
	网购	动词	wǎnggòu	shop online	21
	网上		wǎng shang	online, on the Internet	21
	往	介词	wǎng	toward	18
	微信	名词	wēixìn	WeChat	6
	问	动词	wèn	ask	10
	我	代词	wǒ	I, me	1
	我们	代词	wǒmen	we, us	9

	一点儿	数量词	yìdiǎnr	a little, a bit	19
	银行	名词	yínháng	bank	17
	邮箱	名词	yóuxiāng	email address	6
	有	动词	yǒu	have	6
	有	动词	yǒu	there is	17
	有的	代词	yǒude	some	21
	右边	名词	yòubian	right (side)	16
	月	名词	yuè	month	15
Z	再见	动词	zàijiàn	goodbye, bye	7
	在	动词	zài	be located (in, on, at...)	16
	早上	名词	zǎoshang	morning	2
	怎么	代词	zěnme	how	18
	怎么样	代词	zěnmeyàng	how, how about	21
	站	名词	zhàn	station	17
	找	动词	zhǎo	give change	24
	这	代词	zhè	this	5
	这些	代词	zhèxiē	these	12
	质量	名词	zhìliàng	quality	21
	中国	专有名词	Zhōngguó	China	17
	中国银行	专有名词	Zhōngguó Yínháng	Bank of China	17
	中秋节	专有名词	Zhōngqiū Jié	Mid-Autumn Festival	22
	终点站		zhōngdiǎn zhàn	terminal	23
	转	动词	zhuǎn	transfer	23
	走	动词	zǒu	walk, go	18
	最近	名词	zuìjìn	recently	3
	坐	动词	zuò	travel by (bus, train, plane, etc.)	23

致　谢

衷心感谢以下各方在教材编写及出版过程中提供的各种帮助！

周小兵教授	北京语言大学教师教育学院
彭小川教授	暨南大学华文学院
赵春利教授	暨南大学中文系
吴福焕副教授	新加坡南洋理工大学
刘瑜副教授	美国杨百翰大学
付彦白副主任	北京语言大学出版社国际中文教育事业部
武传霞编辑	北京语言大学出版社国际中文教育事业部
张建编辑	北京语言大学出版社国际中文教育事业部
黄瓒辉副教授	中山大学中文系
方清明教授	华南师范大学国际文化学院
姜有顺副教授	西南大学国际文化学院
张鹏副教授	云南师范大学华文学院
梁珊珊副教授	华南理工大学国际文化学院
张念副教授	中山大学中文系
张绮助理教授	爱尔兰都柏林城市大学应用语言及跨文化研究学院
王红博士	暨南大学华文学院
常芳清老师	暨南大学华文学院
吴晓明老师	暨南大学华文学院
刘丽宁老师	暨南大学华文学院

教材的编写过程还得到了暨南大学和暨南大学华文学院众多领导和同事的大力支持，在此一并深表谢忱！

编者

2023 年 5 月